TRISTRAM SHANDY

A Book for Free Spirits

TWAYNE'S MASTERWORK STUDIES

Robert Lecker, General Editor

TRISTRAM SHANDY

A Book for Free Spirits

Melvyn New

TWAYNE PUBLISHERS • NEW YORK
Maxwell Macmillan Canada • Toronto
Maxwell Macmillan International • New York Oxford Singapore Sydney

823.6
Sterne

Twayne's Masterwork Series No. 132

Tristram Shandy: A Book for Free Spirits
Melvyn New

Twayne Publishers
Macmillan Publishing Company
866 Third Avenue
New York, New York 10022

Maxwell Macmillan Canada, Inc.
1200 Eglinton Avenue East
Suite 200
Don Mills, Ontario M3C 3N1

Library of Congress Cataloging-in-Publication Data

New, Melvyn.
  Tristam Shandy : a book for free spirits / Melvyn New.
    p. cm.—(Twayne's masterwork studies; no. 132)
  Includes bibliographical references and index.
  ISBN 0-8057-8358-X (alk. paper).—ISBN 0-8057-4450-9 (pbk. :
alk. paper)
    1. Sterne, Laurence, 1713–1768. Life and opinions of Tristam
Shandy, gentleman. I. Title. II. Series.
PR3714.T73N44   1994
823'.6—dc20
[B]   94-1654
                                                             CIP

The paper used in this publication meets the minimum requirements of American
National Standard for Information Sciences—Permanence of Paper for Printed Library
Materials. ANSI Z3948-1984.™ ♾

10 9 8 7 6 5 4 3 2 1 (hc)
10 9 8 7 6 5 4 3 2 1 (pb)

Printed in the United States of America

SSB

Contents

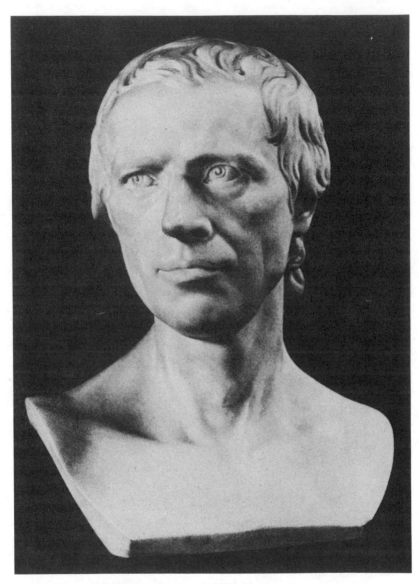

Laurence Sterne, 1766, bust by Joseph Nollekens
Nineteenth-century photography, unattributed

Note on the References and Acknowledgments

The standard scholarly edition of *The Life and Opinions of Tristram Shandy* has been published in three volumes by the University Press of Florida: Volumes I and II, *The Text*, edited by Melvyn New and Joan New (1978), and Volume III, *The Notes*, edited by Melvyn New, with Richard A. Davies and W. G. Day (1984). This edition provides an accurate text based on the first edition of all nine volumes and more than 550 pages of annotations designed to help both first-time readers and advanced scholars. Unfortunately, the cost of the Florida *Tristram* is high; a good college library should have a copy, and it would be worth consulting as one reads the textbook edition the instructor assigns.

I have keyed all quotations from *Tristram Shandy* to the James A. Work edition, published in 1940 by Odyssey Press and currently distributed by Macmillan; the reference will give the volume, chapter, and page number in this edition, followed by a slash and the page number of the Florida edition. This will help students seeking information on a particular passage to locate it easily in the Florida *Notes*. Despite the more than half a century between 1940 and today, Work's notes remain the best available in a textbook edition; his introduction, however, is dated and should be read with caution.

Chronology: Laurence Sterne's Life and Works

1713	Laurence Sterne born on 24 November in Clonmel, Ireland, where his father, Roger, an Ensign in Queen Anne's army, had moved the family after the Treaty of Utrecht in 1713 ended the War of the Spanish Succession.
1723	Departs Ireland to attend school in England under the patronage of his uncle Richard. Laurence never again lives in the same house with his father and mother.
1731	Roger Sterne dies and is buried at his last posting, Port Antonio, Jamaica, 31 July.
1733	Enters Jesus College, Cambridge, where several ancestors had preceded him, including his uncle Richard and Jaques.
1737	Receives his degree in January and takes orders as a clergyman in the Church of England. His first assignment is the parish of St. Ives, Huntingdon, close to Cambridge.
1738–1740	At the beginning of 1738, secures the position of vicar of Sutton-on-the-Forest, a village eight miles north of York; it will remain his home until 1760. In July 1740, receives his Master of Arts degree from Cambridge and begins wooing Elizabeth Lumley, a woman whose virtues stood on her "like quills upon the fretful porcupine."
1741–1757	After a year's courtship, Laurence and Elizabeth are married on 30 March 1741. They have one surviving child, Lydia, born in 1747, and at least one boy who dies at birth or soon thereafter. Sterne's life during these 16 years parallels that of countless eighteenth-century vicars, including the publication of two sermons, one in 1747, the other in 1750.
1756	The Seven Years War begins in Europe and America; this very deadly war, in which all the major European powers are

involved, continues during the writing of the first six volumes of *Tristram Shandy*.

1758   When a local dispute over church prerogatives becomes nasty, satirizes the petty ambitions of all concerned in a short pamphlet entitled *A Political Romance*. Ready for publication in January 1759, it is suddenly suppressed, and only six copies survive.

1759   Having picked up his "creative" pen, will continue writing the remaining nine years of his life. By the end of May, offers Robert Dodsley, the successful London publisher, a manuscript, which Dodsley rejects. Sterne spends the rest of the year revising, and at the end of December, there appears in York the first two volumes of *The Life and Opinions of Tristram Shandy, Gentleman*, copies of which are sent to London.

1760   *Tristram Shandy* is an immediate success. Sterne declares himself the "richest man in Europe" after Dodsley pays him for rights to a second edition and two volumes of his sermons; an arrangement is also made for volumes III and IV. Two more editions of I and II are published this year, as well as volumes I and II of the *Sermons of Mr. Yorick*. In May, returns to a new home in Coxwold, some 15 miles north of York. By late fall is again in London in order to see volumes III and IV through the press (published in January 1761).

1761   Sees volumes V and VI though the press in December (they are dated 1762); changes from Dodsley to a less-established publishing house, Becket and De Hondt, perhaps because they offer more royalties and he is in need of funds; his health is failing, and he must winter in a better climate.

1762–1764   In January 1762, leaves England for the south of France, where he and his family will live until February 1764. His illness is tubercular, with him since college days but now aggravated by his life as a celebrity since 1760. When he finally returns to England in June 1764, by way of Paris, Elizabeth and Lydia stay behind.

1764–1765   In Coxwold, completes volumes VII and VIII, which appear in January 1765. His next project is a second collection of sermons, the manuscript of which he brings to London in October 1765 before departing again for Europe.

1766   Returns to England in June, again without his wife and daughter, but with a new project in mind. Before starting it, however, he writes volume IX, the last volume of *Tristram Shandy*.

Chronology

1767   Volume IX appears in January. Turns to his new work, *A Sentimental Journey*, based largely on his travels in France.

1768   *A Sentimental Journey* is published in two volumes in late February 1768. Still in London, Sterne falls ill and on 18 March, three weeks after the appearance of *Journey*, he dies. David Garrick, the most famous actor of the day, and a friend of Sterne since 1760, writes his epitaph:

> Shall Pride a heap of Sculptur'd Marble raise,
> Some unmourn'd, worthless, titled Fool to praise?
> And shall we not by one poor Grave-stone learn,
> Where Humor, wit and Genius sleep with Sterne?

1769   Three more volumes of Sterne's sermons are published posthumously, under the auspices of his daughter, Lydia, bringing the total number of published sermons to 45, in seven volumes.

LITERARY AND
HISTORICAL CONTEXT

Engraving of a sermon reading from the second edition of *Tristam Shandy*.

1

The Milieu of *Tristram Shandy*

Although *Tristram Shandy* was published in the mid-eighteenth century, its historical horizon might be said to begin some 70 years earlier with the Bloodless Revolution of 1688, in which King William and Queen Mary were invited to England to replace James II, thus ensuring a Protestant succession in Great Britain. This event influenced Sterne's life and writing in several ways. Most important, perhaps, it established the eighteenth-century's perception of the Anglican church as a bastion of moderation and compromise after the religious civil wars of the seventeenth century. Sterne's sense of Anglicanism as a centrist religion between the extremes of reform (Methodism in his own day) and Roman Catholicism takes its rise in the politics of the 1680s. It is no accident, for example, that Tristram is born on the Fifth of November, for that day was joyously celebrated throughout the eighteenth century in commemoration of both the uncovering of the so-called Popish Plot in 1605 to blow up Parliament and the 1688 arrival of William III.

Second, the exile of James II to France reinforced long-standing animosities between France and Great Britain, leading to a century of continental warfare in which these two countries seem always to have been at the center of warring coalitions. From the very beginning, King William is embroiled in wars, one of which climaxes with his great victory at Namur (Belgium) in 1695; the fictional Uncle Toby receives his disabling wound at this battle. Toby's subsequent battles on the bowling green replay William's (and subsequently Queen Anne's) second war, that of the War of the Spanish Succession (1701–13), which was ended by the Treaty of Utrecht in the same year Sterne was born. Keeping in mind that the world of Toby and Trim is set in these early years, some two generations prior to the writing of *Tristram Shandy*, is important. Also worth noting is that Sterne's father was himself a soldier; and, that, from 1756 to 1763, Britain and France were again engaged in a bloody war, the Seven Years War, on the continent and in America.

Finally, the events of 1688 created the Stuart "claim" to the throne, a half century of efforts by the heirs of James II to reassert the family's rights in Britain, culminating in 1745 with a landing in Scotland and a short-lived rebellion. Because the invading army crossed the northern border of England, Yorkshire found itself on the invasion route, and both patriotism and anti-Catholic feelings reached a fever pitch. It is perhaps a sign of the political stability of the eighteenth century that this incursion caused so great an uproar and so little effect (except on the Highlanders of Scotland, whose clan system was decimated in the aftermath). Fifteen years later, in *Tristram Shandy*, Sterne pillories Dr. John Burton of York, who had been active in the Stuart cause, in the figure of Dr. Slop; the anti-Catholicism of the portrait is clearly a remnant of feelings generated by the '45, as the last Stuart uprising in 1745 came to be called.

In thinking about Sterne's culture and milieu, however, one must remember that he lived his adult life a week's travel from London, on the other side of a cultural divide certainly as great as that which today separates urban from rural life. While Pope and Swift could see themselves in the 1720s and 1730s involved in a national struggle against the powerful Prime Minister, Robert Walpole, Sterne's politics were local and provincial. Lewis Perry Curtis and, more recently, Kenneth Monkman have provided interesting evidence of Sterne's journalistic involvement in local elections and the '45,[1] but we are still left with an overwhelming feeling that Sterne's life and intellect were little touched by the march of history as the century progressed. Quite the contrary, we have many indications that in the 1740s and 1750s, Sterne's life was locked into an unchanging stability that ignored or bypassed the sense of radical change that others living in the middle of the century might well have felt. He struggled, unsuccessfully, for advancement in the church; he engaged in local politics, until its pettiness prompted him to desist. He tried his hand at farming to supplement an inadequate income; he and Elizabeth raised a daughter, with whom he seems to have been particularly close. He wrote sermons and preached every week in his parish church; and sometimes he took his turn preaching in the magnificent York Cathedral.

Of course, this stability and this isolation can be overstated. York was the cultural center of northern England, the seat of the Archbishop of York, the second-ranking churchman in the Anglican world. The town had a theater and booksellers, access to London periodicals and newspapers. Scientific improvements in agriculture, medicine, and technology would certainly reach York in a timely fashion. Moreover, Sterne seems to have taken pride in his own accomplishments in two cultural spheres, music (he played the violin or bass viol or both) and painting; he seems to have been familiar not only with the works but also the theories of both William Hogarth (1697–1764) and Sir Joshua Reynolds (1723–92), two of the age's outstanding painters. He also seems to have had an interest in the theater, as numerous allusions in *Tristram Shandy* attest.

Sterne's reading, however, offers us our best insight into his cultural milieu, and here our sense of his relative isolation is most strongly felt. The literary tradition with which Sterne is most usually associated is that of the novelists Daniel Defoe (1660–1731), Henry Fielding (1707–54), Samuel Richardson (1689–1761), and Tobias Smollett (1721–71). Interestingly, Sterne never mentions the first three—and Smollett comes to his attention as a travel-writer and editor of the *Critical Review*, rather than as a novelist. Sterne's literary interests seem clearly to point to earlier generations of writers, Jonathan Swift (1667–1745) and Alexander Pope (1688–1744) in the era preceding his, and even further back, into the Renaissance,

François Rabelais (1494–1533) and Michel de Montaigne (1533–92), Miguel de Cervantes (1547–1616), and Robert Burton (1577–1640). These are the authors with whom Sterne asks to be compared and the authors with whom his contemporaries were most likely to compare him. Similarly, while the avant garde philosophical readers of midcentury Britain would be studying David Hume (1711–76), Sterne seems to have remained fixed on John Locke (1632–1704). I explore reasons for these predilections in the course of my reading of *Tristram Shandy*, but at this point it is simply worth keeping in mind that within the history of literature, Sterne's interests seem uniformly directed toward the past rather than toward what was happening in his own day.

One additional aspect of Sterne's cultural milieu must be given some attention, the rise of the eighteenth-century phenomenon known as *sentimentalism*.[2] In many ways, this movement spans the entire century. A reaction to the bawdiness of the Restoration comedy of William Wycherley (1640–1716) and William Congreve (1670–1729) led, at the beginning of the eighteenth century, to a mode of comedy that stressed virtue and conjugal devotion; by midcentury, sentimental comedy dominated the theater, and the stage was filled with incredibly pious young men and women, their sexual appetites effectively buried under layers of heartfelt verbiage. In poetry, the satiric mode of Dryden, Pope, and Swift had been replaced by the emotion-drenched odes of William Collins (1721–59); in both poetry and fiction, the mark of excellence (the author's *and* the reader's) had become a single teardrop upon the page.

Sentimentalism as a literary movement was symptomatic of a much larger cultural event: the eighteenth century was a watershed for the pervasive role of Christianity in moral thinking. To oversimplify, prior to Sterne's century, little if any claim could be sustained for human self-sufficiency in questions of morality; the human conscience, along with the human will, was considered fallen and hence depraved, and our goodness was owed to the grace of God and His powerful intervention in our daily lives. The mediation of the church, reflective of Christ's necessary and saving sacrifice, was absolutely required to ensure moral conduct. By the end of the eighteenth century, this notion had lost much of its potency. The roots of the "new morality" have been traced to many sources; here, let one name suffice, Anthony Ashley Cooper, the Third Earl of Shaftesbury (1671–1713), whose *Characteristics of Men, Manners, Opinions, Times* (1711) gathers many of the justifications posited for a morality based upon the innate tastes and capacities of the individual person. Sterne's relationship to Shaftesbury—indeed, to the sentimental tradition—will receive a great deal of attention herein, particularly in chapter 7.

When Sterne published the first two volumes of *Tristram Shandy* in December 1759, he had been preceded within the year by three other significant new publications. The first was Adam Smith's *Theory of Moral Sentiments*, which attempted the most complete codification of the possibilities of a morality without religious mediation since Shaftesbury's similar effort. It seems no accident that the author of the economic masterpiece, *Wealth of Nations* (1776), began his career with a work on moral theory; indeed, it is a strong indication of the probability that the historical, cultural, and economic theories of any society are written under the aegis of whatever moral theory that society embraces, an observation central to understanding *Tristram Shandy*.

The second work published in 1759 was Voltaire's *Candide*, a work Sterne alludes to in the very first volume of *Tristram Shandy*. Voltaire's satire on optimism and the bloodthirsty history of humankind reverberates in many ways in Sterne's work, but above all it serves to remind us that the march of economic and social progressiveness, with which the eighteenth century is so often associated, did not proceed unopposed by some thinkers. It also might remind us that Sterne's "historical context" must not be confined to British shores but extends to the continent as well; his argument with Shaftesburian morality, for example, seems clearly to be mirrored in Voltaire's similar argument, in *Candide*, against the moral enthusiasms of Leibniz and Rousseau.

Finally, Samuel Johnson (1709–84) published *Rasselas* in 1759; we know Sterne was acquainted with the work because he suggested to Dodsley that his *Tristram* be published in the same format. There is no better entrée into *Tristram Shandy* than Rasselas's confrontation with the riddles and mysteries, the chances and changes, of human experience; with the futility of all human systems and dogmas, and the dangerous prevalence of the imagination (the hobby-horse). That Sterne's work can be richly comprehended within a context provided by Samuel Johnson is, to my mind, not without significance; while the label *Age of Johnson* for the period of English literature between 1740 and 1800 is, like all taxonomic labels, more a convenience than a truth, it does seem fair to say that however we might define the "tradition, culture, and milieu" of the second half of the eighteenth century in Britain, Johnson is at its center. If nothing else, *Rasselas* and *Candide* remind us that not every fiction is a novel, and indeed, that in 1759, the year in which *Tristram Shandy* first saw the light of day, two other brilliant works of literature appeared in which both plot and character are clearly subordinated to the ideas being critically explored by their authors.

2

The Importance of *Tristram Shandy*

Tristram Shandy has been considered "important" for more than 200 years because its readers have thought it was "important." In logic, this is called the fallacy of circular reasoning, but it is the best I can do without lapsing into predictable pieties or windy obfuscations. It does help, perhaps, to recall that among those readers considering *Tristram* "important" have been the most "important" writers (but, again, the logic is circular) of the last two centuries in Europe: Diderot and Voltaire, Coleridge and Scott, Goethe and Tolstoy, Nietzsche, Proust, Joyce, Virginia Woolf, and Thomas Mann. In recent years, writers as diverse as the Indian author Salman Rushdie in *Midnight's Children*, the Spanish author Juan Goytisolo in *Juan the Landless* (*Juan sin terre*), and the Mexican author Carlos Fuentes in *Christopher Unborn* (*Cristóbal Nonato*), have all written major fictions derived from *Tristram Shandy*. If we think of writing as a way of commenting on what we read, some of our best writers clearly consider *Tristram Shandy* an important work, one worthy of extensive commentary.

Can we define a common ground for the many readers—from different times and cultures—who have considered *Tristram Shandy* important? We might try to do so, if only to avoid the common error of declaring the work open to—indeed inviting—every one's individual interpretation, all of which are deemed of equal value. I would begin, I think, with the notion that Sterne reinforces a great Renaissance tradition of "unknowingness" (with roots deep enough to touch Aristophanes and Solomon), a tradition under dire challenge in his century and ours, the challenge of rationalism. For the rationalist, the possibility that one can encounter a problem or contradiction and fail to resolve it is most unsettling; reason, logic, human progress, and mental well-being, all suggest the need to resolve contradictions, make determinations, reconcile all conflicts as part of some larger and better design.

This faith in the systematic resolution of problematic conflicts (the practice of science) became the dominant mode of thinking in Europe during the eighteenth century and continued to dominate in the nineteenth century and through much of this century as well. Sterne's importance has been to keep alive an opposition to this new drummer, a stubborn way of looking at contradictions within a context (Christian and skeptical, as each seeks reinforcement from the other) of human limitations and worldly complexities. Resolution and positiveness are the tempting and inevitable vices of Sterne's worldview; suspension and doubt, its difficult, if not impossible, virtues.

And it is not merely contradictions and puzzlements in character or subject matter that *Tristram* illustrates; indeed, far more important is the contradiction of Sterne's art, the carefully crafted impression of carelessness and abandon. Sterne is the eminently sane writer pretending to be mad (a formal lesson he learned from Cervantes and Swift), one of the primary aesthetic defenses of modern art and artists against an insane world. In a world gone mad with the infinite hypocrisies of "problem-solving" (which Sterne will characterize as *gravity*, Swift as *hypocrisy*, but fascists as *final solutions*), the artist must insist, in John Keats's famous formula, on the vast energies and joys to be found in the infinite contradictions of "negative capability": "At once it struck me what quality went to form a man of achievement, especially in literature, and which Shakespeare possessed so enormously—I mean negative capability, that is when a man is capable of being in uncertainties, mysteries, doubts, without any irritable reaching after fact and reason."[1] Because every fiber of our being cries out to resolve the painful (threatening) mysteries surrounding us, the artist whose work embodies a countervailing tendency has much to show us. Sterne's ever-increasing reputation, which has grown perhaps more than that of any other eighteenth-century author in the past half century, strongly suggests that modern readers and writers alike feel an urgent need to understand and cultivate Sterne's antirationalism as this most rational—and murderous—century draws to a close.

This is the lasting importance of *Tristram Shandy* to my mind, what makes it a book necessary to teach in college classrooms and necessary to return to repeatedly as an adult, most especially when we are confronted—as we all are, daily and inevitably—with those who are absolutely certain in their judgments and who insist that we mount and gallop behind them. Then again, insofar as we are all mounted and galloping on one hobby-horse or another, *Tristram Shandy* is a book for everyone, and precisely that awareness of self-implication I have just manifested is perhaps the final and certainly the best lesson we can carry away from a reading of Laurence Sterne.

3

Tristram Shandy among the Critics

From the outset, Sterne took a lively interest in the reception of *Tristram Shandy*, perhaps sharing Tristram's ironic view that he wrote "not to be fed but to be famous." Thus, when he published his first two volumes in York, he omitted the damning evidence of provincial printing from the title page; and when he sent copies down to London, he put them into the hands of a young singer, along with a letter celebrating the work, for delivery to David Garrick. These maneuvers worked beyond Sterne's best hopes; within weeks, he was in London signing a lucrative contract with Robert Dodsley for the second edition and getting the famous artist William Hogarth to provide a frontispiece. Indeed, in his heady success, Sterne made a major blunder. In May 1760, four months after his "triumph," he tried to "cash in" by publishing two volumes of sermons (hastily scraped together from his drawer) under the name "Mr. Yorick"; Sterne may have wanted fame, but after a lifetime on a country vicar's stipend, he seems to have had a healthy interest in fortune as well. The virtuous howled over sermons published under a "jester's" name, and Sterne's audience returned to *Tristram Shandy* ready to condemn from a tasteless clergyman what they had enjoyed as a Rabelaisian, Cervantic, Swiftian jaunt from an anonymous genius.

Tristram Shandy *among the Critics*

Clearly, the reception of a literary work is more complicated than might at first appear; public taste is always more—and less—than an aesthetic (or disinterested) judgment. Hence, among some famous eighteenth-century figures there was almost immediate disagreement in the first few years following *Tristram*'s appearance. Garrick immediately liked the work, as did James Boswell. Garrick's closest acquaintance in London was Samuel Johnson, whom Boswell would meet three years later. But Johnson, when he thought about *Tristram Shandy* at all, did so only to dismiss it: "Nothing odd will do long; *Tristram Shandy* did not last." And yet, David Hume, the great eighteenth-century skeptical philosopher—who exchanged pleasantries with Sterne in France in 1764—writing in 1773 declares *Tristram Shandy* "the best Book, that has been writ by any Englishman these thirty Years . . . , bad as it is. A Remark which may astonish you; but which you will find true on Reflection."[1] Likewise, Thomas Jefferson wrote in 1787: "The writings of Sterne, particularly, form the best course of morality that ever was written" (Howes, 216).

These comments have something of English reserve about them; the best German writers in the late eighteenth century were far more exuberant. C. M. Wieland, an important German poet, was a very early supporter: "I confess . . . that Sterne is almost the only author in the world whom I regard with a kind of awed admiration. I shall study his book as long as I live and will still not have studied it enough. I know of nothing else in which there is so much genuine Socratic wisdom . . . , so much healthy judgment, combined with so much wit and genius" (Howes, 424).

But it is Goethe, the greatest of German authors, who best expresses his nation's adoration of Sterne.

> Yorick–Sterne was the most beautiful spirit that ever lived; who reads him immediately feels free and beautiful. . . . He felt a definite hatred for seriousness because it is didactic and dogmatic and very easily becomes pedantic, qualities which he despised. Thus his antipathy toward terminology. In the most varied studies and reading he uncovered everywhere the inadequate and the absurd. . . .

He jokes very graciously about the contradictions which make his condition ambiguous. . . .
I still have not met his equal in the broad field of literature. (Howes, 433–35)

Those familiar with Goethe will realize that he admired in Sterne what he believed to be his own greatest virtues, but that hardly disqualifies his comments from being important and legitimate observations. Indeed, they serve as a handy guide to the reading of *Tristram Shandy* I offer in the chapters that follow.

There was also enthusiasm in France. Denis Diderot, the Encyclopédiste who would later write an important commentary on Sterne by way of his own satiric fiction, *Jacques le fataliste*, comments in 1762: "This book so mad, so wise, and so gay is the English Rabelais. . . . I can't give you a better idea of it than by calling it a universal satire" (Howes, 385). Voltaire calls Sterne "England's second Rabelais" (Swift being the first), although, interestingly enough, the author of *Candide* took umbrage at times with Sterne's bawdy.

Because new and quite often elaborate editions of *Tristram Shandy* were published almost every year from Sterne's death in 1768 to the end of the nineteenth century, we can assume a certain amount of public reading taking place. Still, noting that a collection entitled *The Beauties of Sterne: including all his pathetic tales, and most distinguished observations on life. Selected for the Heart of Sensibility* went through some 15 editions before the end of the century, we might also suspect this public of harboring a rather one-sided version of Sterne, shaped in large part by the popularity of *A Sentimental Journey*, and by the desire to avoid the "moral questions" first raised by the *Sermons of Mr. Yorick*. On the continent, particularly in nineteenth-century Germany, Sterne became the patron saint of sensibility, a name that could hardly be invoked without a tear trickling down the cheek. In England, C. R. Leslie painted a "warm" portrait of Uncle Toby trying to find the speck in Widow Wadman's eye; it reappears as a popular engraving, as ceramicware, and on probably thousands of crockery jar lids. One might suspect that Victorian males read a different *Tristram*

Shandy than Victorian females, but society seems to have made it possible for both to continue encountering and enjoying the work.

In nineteenth-century France, Honoré de Balzac complimented Sterne by using the image of Trim's waving his stick as a gesture of liberty (IX.4) to preface the many volumes of his *Comédie Humaine*; and back in Germany, Heinrich Heine ranked Sterne above his countryman, Jean Paul (Richter), because "Sterne was the greater poet. . . . Sometimes, when his soul is most deeply agitated with tragic emotion . . . then, to his own astonishment, the merriest, most mirth-provoking words will flutter from his lips."[2] Like Goethe, Heine finds in Sterne what he hopes to accomplish himself. We begin to understand the meaning of the Shandean hobby-horse when we see how these great writers confront Sterne's writings with their own various strengths and weaknesses, likes and dislikes, whims and obsessions. To be sure, readers who are not great writers will also read themselves into a literary work.

Among English Romantics, Coleridge engaged in the most extensive discussions about Sterne, although his approval was mixed and his comments—largely borrowed from the German humorist and theorist Jean Paul—at times confused. Beginning with the notion that humor is created by contemplating the finite in reference to the infinite, Coleridge notes that "humorous writers, therefore, as Sterne in particular, delight to end in nothing, or a direct contradiction. . . . Hence in humor the little is made great, and the great little, in order to destroy both, because all is equal in contrast with the infinite." Coleridge also speaks of the hobby-horse leading us to respect the disinterestedness of the rider, while acknowledging the "hollowness and farce of the world, and its disproportion to the godlike within us" (Howes, 353–54). I shall have several occasions in my later chapters to return to Coleridge's (and Jean Paul's) romantic reading of Sterne's irony.

We cannot linger any longer in the past except to note that Dickens must surely have had Uncle Toby in mind when he created Mr. Pickwick—and, indeed, the hobby-horse looms behind literally hundreds of his characters; and that Tolstoy labels Sterne his "favorite writer," acknowledging in particular his "tremendous talent for narration."[3] In order to close the nineteenth century, however, we should return to Germany, where the voice of our own age was being heard in the brilliant and disturbing writings of Friedrich Nietzsche. In *Assorted Opinions and Maxims* (1879), later published as part of the second volume of *Human, All Too Human* (1886), Nietzsche devoted a long section to Sterne, titled, *"The most liberated writer."* Although I return to the passage for an extensive analysis in chapter 9, I want to quote it here at some length because the reading of *Tristram Shandy* offered in the following pages takes its impetus as well as its conclusion from Nietzsche's admiration; the echoes of Goethe's comments should be readily apparent.

> How, in a book for free spirits [the subtitle of *Human, All Too Human*], should there be no mention of Laurence Sterne, whom Goethe honoured as the most liberated spirit of his century! Let us content ourselves here simply with calling him the most liberated spirit of all time, in comparison with whom all others seem stiff, square, intolerant and boorishly direct. What is to be praised in him is not the closed and transparent but the "endless melody": if with this expression we may designate an artistic style in which the fixed form is constantly being broken up, displaced, transposed back into indefiniteness, so that it signifies one thing and at the same time another. Sterne is the great master of *ambiguity*—this word taken in a far wider sense than is usually done when it is accorded only a sexual signification. The reader who demands to know exactly what Sterne really thinks of a thing, whether he is making a serious or a laughing face, must be given up for lost: for he knows how to encompass both in a *single* facial expression; he likewise knows how, and even wants to be in the right and in the wrong at the same time, to knot together profundity and farce. . . . [H]is aphorisms are at the same time an expression of an attitude of irony towards all sententiousness, his antipathy to seriousness is united with a tendency to be unable to regard anything merely superficially. Thus he produces in the right reader a feeling of uncertainty as to whether one is walking, standing or lying: a feeling, that is, closely related to floating. . . . Such an ambiguousness become flesh and soul, such a free-spiritedness in every fibre and muscle of the body, have as he possessed these qualities perhaps been possessed by no other man.[4]

Tristram Shandy *among the Critics*

Except, of course, by Nietzsche himself—at least in the mirror he here holds up for his own self-portrait. Nietzsche's reading of Sterne is a self-examination. The reader he believes Sterne requires is the ideal reader for his own writing; and his description of Sterne is simply one more effort by Nietzsche to define his own character to the world. Our own interpretation will accept the challenge, not so much of understanding Nietzsche, perhaps, but of Sterne's meaning for a modern world permeated in immeasurable ways by the Nietzschean presence.

Reading eighteenth-century novels in the twentieth century has turned into a quite odd activity, most especially since the advent of cinema, radio, and television has offered such pervasive (and persuasive) alternate modes of popular leisure-time activity. Today, it is difficult to imagine someone reading *Tristram Shandy* for the first time *outside* the college classroom; and while such generalizations are made to be gainsaid, it does seem evident that by far the largest audience for Sterne today is composed of students for whom his works are "required reading." Hence, reprintings of *Tristram* in the last 50 years have been almost exclusively textbook editions. The "critical reception" of *Tristram Shandy* is now almost solely in the hands of those who "read" in order to write and teach (the scholar-teacher), and the book is read primarily within a process of literary instruction. While this academic experience certainly exposes more people to the work than Sterne could ever have imagined, we may yet come to regret a culture in which we no longer read works of the past independent of instructional (and hence interpretative) duress.

Courses in eighteenth-century English literature, at least in the United States, seem early in the century to have divided the canon between novels on the one hand, and poetry, drama, and nonfiction on the other. *Tristram Shandy*, which is long and in prose, is most often read with the novelists, alongside Defoe, Fielding, Richardson, and Smollett. Insofar as the dominant critical approach toward these authors in the twentieth century have been to explore the rise and development of the novel in their hands, approaches to Sterne for much of the century have almost always followed this reasoning. The novel begins with Defoe's first halting steps and develops, so the argument goes, with ever-increasing sophistication—and a few unfortunate

17

missteps—to the flowering of the genre from, roughly, 1830 to 1930. For some, Sterne is one of the missteps, "irresponsible (and nasty) trifling" according to F. R. Leavis's footnote dismissal of *Tristram* in his dominating study of English fiction, *The Great Tradition*.[5] For others, however, *Tristram Shandy* is the first antinovel or metanovel, undoing by self-consciousness the development of realism, plot construction, and character motivation supposedly under way after Defoe. For these critics, Sterne is, in his self-conscious narration, his defiance of design, his psychological inquiries, the forerunner of more experimental authors such as James Joyce and Samuel Beckett.

Thus, while Sterne was being taken quite seriously in the early part of the century, the subject of an extensive biography by Wilbur L. Cross and a definitive collection of his correspondence edited by Lewis Perry Curtis,[6] one should also note that, as a novelist, his status as a canonical figure remained precarious because so much of his work seemed extraneous to the "serious" development of realistic fiction. Indeed, the eighteenth-century novel itself had a tentative grasp, at best, on "greatness," for critics tended to treat Defoe, Richardson, and Fielding much as they treated Thomas Gray and William Collins—as weak and flawed precursors of the achievements to come (that is, of the European realistic novel in the first instance, of romantic poetry in the second). In this weak light, Sterne was almost always praised for only two accomplishments: his sentimental (warm) characterizations and his attention to physical (domestic) detail. But he was condemned for a host of failures, including, of course, his lack of plot and serious intent.

In 1954, John Traugott's *Tristram Shandy's World: Sterne's Philosophical Rhetoric* changed all this.[7] First, Traugott provided "philosophical" depth to Sterne by insisting that *Tristram Shandy* was a major challenge to the most influential philosophical treatise of the eighteenth century, a critique of John Locke's "rationalism" in *Essay Concerning Human Understanding*. Second, this critique, the like of which would not be seen again until Kant, was shown to be infinitely complex, indeed quite often hidden from the uninitiated reader. Traugott demonstrated that *Tristram Shandy* could no longer be read without the guidance of scholar-critics; the text we might read as an amateur had little bearing on the "real" meaning hidden behind a complex metaphysical and epistemological struggle with Locke.

Third, Traugott gave us a Sterne who was "one of us," a modern existentialist, alienated and absurd, but confronting the abyss with sentiment and fellow-feeling, hence transcending after all. Moreover, and closely connected to the existential-sentimental nexus, Traugott convinced us that *Tristram Shandy* was a book of vital moral import—of a secular sort. Sterne had freed himself from old-fashioned notions of morality (that is, from Christianity), but sentimentality was found to contain a rich lode of moralisms, masking themselves as problems of communication and emotional expressiveness. Finally, by inventing "rhetoric" as the generic label for *Tristram*, Traugott attempted to free it from the company of the novelists where it had not fared well. By suggesting that the work was *sui generis*, a genre by itself, Traugott allowed us to look at it without our preconceptions of what novels should be; and by insisting upon the distinction between Swift's "philosophical rhetoric" and Sterne's, he was able to extol a moral stance far more comfortable to the modern mind than Swift's old-fashioned Christian pessimism.

Traugott's reading has dominated Sterne criticism since it appeared 40 years ago, excepting only that he failed to persuade critics to accept *Tristram Shandy* as a "rhetoric"; instead, they continue to treat it as a novel, but now as one informed by philosophical concerns, derived from Locke, and anticipating Marcel Proust and Joyce. The fact that it was being taught in eighteenth-century *novel* courses was the primary reason for this insistence; a second reason had to do with the "liberal" or "progressive" or "modernist" bias such a reading provides. Scores of interpretations were produced, all pointing in exactly the same direction: Sterne's *novel*, critics argued, is an exploration of the epistemological fallacies inherent in Locke's philosophy, and the loving and touching portrayal of a domestic or personal evasion of those fallacies through nonverbal processes of communication. As a corollary, Sterne and Tristram are one and the same, and Sterne is exploring, as Proust and Joyce and other modernists would later do, the workings of his own mind, both as the remembrance of past experience and within the current context of his writing a book called

Tristram Shandy. Between Traugott and James Swearingen's phenomenological study in 1977, or Wolfgang Iser's dreary rehash in 1988,[8] differences in details are perhaps found, but none in fundamental approach; all argue within a context determined by the powerful arguments of Traugott.

Two paths of a counterargument to Traugott were actually in print when *Tristram Shandy's World* appeared, D. W. Jefferson's essay on the Renaissance tradition of "learned wit," as it reappears in Sterne's work, and Wayne Booth's "The Self-Conscious Narrator in Comic Fiction before *Tristram Shandy*," which undercut Traugott's *sui generis* argument and also put into doubt the conflation of Sterne and Tristram as one indistinguishable voice.[9] Building on their work, John M. Stedmond's *The Comic Art of Laurence Sterne* (1967) and my own *Laurence Sterne as Satirist* (1969),[10] while offering ultimately quite different readings, both opened questions of genre, of Sterne's debt to the Renaissance and to writers such as Swift, of Sterne's Anglicanism and its role in *Tristram Shandy*, and of the attitude toward sentimentalism in the work. Stedmond's approach was to seek a compromise between Traugott's reading and his own; mine was a more rigorous (many said "rigid") formalist approach to *Tristram* as a satire on duncery in the Pope–Swift tradition. Neither work, however, was able significantly to dislodge Traugott's dominance in the 1970s.

The 1980s, on the other hand, produced several indications of the waning of the existential-sentimental approach, not the least of which is the replacement of existentialism by numerous other *-isms* within the critical community. Moreover, the postmodernist tendency to downplay works and authors in favor of critics, texts, and paradigms has opened the study of literature—not just *Tristram Shandy*— to a host of new readings within marxist models, feminist models, deconstructive models, psychological models, and the like. The most interesting such readings have had to do with a reexamination of the women in *Tristram Shandy* and Sterne's attitude toward them. For several critics, this has resulted in separating the clearly misogynist views of the Shandy males from Sterne's own view.[11]

The second indication that Traugott's grip is finally being loosened is the widening reexamination of Sterne's contemporary context and his relationship to preceding authors. Hence, even in a deconstructive study such as Jonathan Lamb's *Sterne's Fiction and the Double Principle,* Lamb is intent upon reexamining Sterne's interest in Montaigne, Hogarth, and Addison and Steele—and intent upon rereading these figures in a light different from that cast by literary history in the past.[12] While it is true that postmodernist readings often seem detached from the author and the work, it is also worth observing that the universal skepticism undergirding postmodernism often results in undoing reified critical commonplaces by exposing the cultural biases that produced them. Whether under the aegis of new historicism, marxism, feminism, or deconstruction, the thrust of present-day literary criticism is to challenge "received wisdom."

Abetting this challenge, I believe, are the 550 pages of annotations to *Tristram Shandy* published as volume III of the Florida edition in 1984. The notes help to locate Sterne among his own historical and cultural markers, but more significantly they argue, collectively, an essential difference between novels, the narrative emphasis of which limits the amount of annotation required to elucidate them, and satires, which have always required extensive annotation because of the satirist's reliance upon parody and burlesque, upon contemporary targets and issues, and upon the valorizing effects of cross-reference, allusion, and recognizable imitation. This study will depend heavily at several points upon the findings gathered in the Florida *Notes.*

When James Joyce wanted to explain *Finnegans Wake,* his most experimental fiction, he invoked Sterne: "Time and the river and the mountain are the real heroes of my book. Yet the elements are exactly what every novelist might use: man and woman, birth, childhood, night, sleep, marriage, prayer, death. There is nothing paradoxical about this. Only I am trying to build as many planes of narrative with a single esthetic purpose. Did you ever read Laurence Sterne?"[13] And when Thomas Mann tried to explain the achievement of his great *Joseph* saga, he also invoked Sterne: "There is a symptom for the innate character of a work, for the category toward which it strives . . . : that is the reading matter which the author prefers and which he considers helpful while working on it. . . . Well then, such strengthening reading during the last Joseph years was provided by two books:

Laurence Sterne's 'Tristram Shandy' and Goethe's 'Faust' . . . and in this connection it was a pleasure for me to know that Goethe had held Sterne in very high esteem."[14] Insofar as literary criticism is always a confused and conflicted reflection of *current* critical interests and methodologies, ending our discussion of the critical reception of *Tristram Shandy* with these comments of Joyce and Mann is useful. That many of the most important authors of our age have found their art and their egos reflected in Sterne's work and have, reciprocally, reflected his work in their own writing, is perhaps the most important observation one can make about Sterne's "critical reception." The awesome authority that accrues to great achievement is at least a temporary refuge from the conflicts of opinions, prejudices, and insights that mark the fate of every significant literary work.

A READING

Engraving of the Christening from the first edition of *Tristam Shandy*.

4

Introduction

What is to be praised in [Sterne] is . . . the "endless melody": . . . an artistic style in which the fixed form is constantly being broken up, displaced, transposed back into indefiniteness.

(*Human*, 238)

The model for the following "reading" of *Tristram Shandy* owes its rather strange format to a method used by Stuart Gilbert in his study of James Joyce's *Ulysses*.[1] Gilbert headed each of his chapters (one for each episode of *Ulysses*) with a list of general categories and the episode's specific reflections of them. For example, here are the six categories he uses most often, along with the specifics provided for Episodes 4 ("Calypso") and 10 ("The Wandering Rocks") respectively:

Scene	*The House*	*The Streets*
Hour	*8 A.M.*	*3 P.M.*
Organ	*Kidney*	*Blood*
Art	*Economics*	*Mechanics*
Symbol	*Nymph*	*Citizens*
Technic	*Narrative (mature)*	*Labyrinth*

What appeals to me in so rigid a schematization is precisely its blatant artificiality. It calls attention to the act of "reading" as an organizing, demarcating, and ultimately limiting exercise.

Much recent literary criticism has tried very hard to disguise this assertion of power over the text, but in fact all critical reading seems heavily structured, especially in the hands of professionals whose trade is the production of interpretation. I shall, of course, be practicing that trade myself; what follows is a highly personal response to *Tristram Shandy*—indeed five responses with, I hope, unresolved contradictions. Rather than pretending to subordinate myself to Sterne's text by pursuing his work volume by volume as if I were simply recovering his process, I offer five chapters that quite obviously pursue my own agenda. Each chapter is headed by the same list of seven general categories and for each category, I offer an aspect of *Tristram Shandy* to be discussed in the chapter; these seven aspects are more or less tied together under the rubric of the chapter title, always a common noun. In addition, I begin and end each chapter with a quotation from Nietzsche, whose high praise of *Tristram Shandy* has already been chronicled. Nietzsche comments somewhere, speaking as a male, that if truth is imaged as a woman (as does Tristram: "the bottom of the well, where TRUTH keeps her little court" [IV.S.T. 257/306]), we had better learn how to dance. This reading of *Tristram Shandy* attempts a dance with Sterne to the music of Nietzsche. Perhaps at the conclusion we will have at least a better understanding of why Nietzsche labeled Sterne "the most liberated spirit of all time."

I have kept in mind that this volume is not intended for other scholars, and have tried, therefore, to keep my scholarly apparatus (citations and notes) to a minimum. For errant scholars who do stumble on it, I will acknowledge what will quickly be apparent to them, namely, that several of my arguments herein have appeared in more scholarly form elsewhere over the years. I do not believe this self-borrowing is overly extensive, but it might serve to suggest that what appears here to be unscholarly assertion has had the benefit of documentation in appropriate forums.

As for the students to whom this study of *Tristram Shandy* is directed, I can give no better advice as you begin the task of understanding Sterne than this challenge from Nietzsche's *Twilight of the Idols*: "One is *fruitful* only at the cost of being rich in contradictions; one remains *young* only on condition the soul does not relax, does not long for peace."[2]

5

Satire

Character   *Yorick*
Foil   *Tristram*
Incident   *Yorick's Life and Death*
Document   *The Abuses of Conscience Sermon*
Activity   *Judging*
Image   *The Black Page*
-Ism   *Fideism*

Man is difficult to discover, most of all to himself; the spirit often
tells lies about the soul. The Spirit of Gravity is the cause of that.[1]

Laurence Sterne was 46 years old when he sat down to write *Tristram
Shandy*. He had spent much of his adult life, from 1738 onward, serv-
ing as the Anglican vicar of a rural parish, Sutton-on-the-Forest, a village some eight miles north of York. During this long period he had
engaged sporadically in political writing in local newspapers and had
committed to paper some of his Sunday sermons; indeed, he had local-
ly published two of them, delivered on special occasions, one of which
would reappear verbatim as the sermon Trim reads in volume II of
Tristram. But had Sterne died in his forty-fifth year, he would have

done so unnoticed by the world then—and certainly unrecognized by
it today. Hence, 1759 was truly an annus mirabilis, a year of sudden
and surprising achievement that carried Sterne from his country pulpit
to the center of London's literary life. How did it happen?

In January 1759, a pamphlet entitled *A Political Romance* was
being readied for publication in York. It was a local satire, based upon
incidents in an ongoing dispute over prerogatives within the York
church establishment; so ridiculous and petty did Sterne, its author,
make his fellow clergymen appear, that the pamphlet was suppressed.
Perhaps the writing of *Romance*, perhaps its suppression, gave Sterne
the impetus to continue in a creative vein. The available evidence
points to a second effort that was again satiric, an attempt to imitate
Alexander Pope's *Peri Bathous; or, The Art of Sinking in Poetry* (1727),
except that the subject matter was sermon-writing. The first two chapters of this project, the "Fragment in the Manner of Rabelais," are
extant. In them, the erstwhile preacher Homenas, surrounded by
Rabelaisian comrades, Panurge, Gymnast, Triboulet, attempts to write
his weekly sermon by raiding his library; "*Alass* poor *Homenas*,"
Sterne intones, when he falls from the balcony.[2]

And so one enters the world of *Tristram Shandy*, in which one
certain guise for the author is the village parson, Yorick, a name with
which Sterne felt extremely comfortable, using it again when his sermons were published under the title *The Sermons of Mr. Yorick* (1760,
1766), and yet again when he named the protagonist of *A Sentimental
Journey* (1768). If we know our Shakespeare, we know the name is
that of the Danish king's jester, but a jester whose sole appearance in
Hamlet occurs as a skull to be contemplated in the famous gravedig-
gers' scene: "Alas, poor Yorick! I knew him, Horatio. A fellow of infinite jest. . . ."[3] The country parson from *York* and *Yorick*'s skull come
together in the portrait of Yorick on his broken-down horse meditat-
ing "as delightfully *de vanitate mundi et fugâ sæculi* ["on the vanity of
the world and the swift passing of time"], as with the advantage of a
death's head before him" (I.10.20/20).

Sterne invokes here the medieval tradition of *memento mori*, the
use of various devices, often a human skull, to keep death uppermost
in a Christian's mind. He had used the Latin tag to similar purpose in

his sermon "Eternal Advantages of Religion": "the shortness and
uncertainty of life . . . are meditations so obvious . . . that it is aston-
ishing how it was possible, at any time, for mortal man to have his
head full of any thing else?—And yet . . . as wisely as we all . . . philos-
ophize *de contemptu mundi & fugâ sæculi*;—yet . . . there are multi-
tudes who seem to take aim at nothing higher. . . ."[4] Yorick's presence
in *Tristram Shandy* serves to remind us of ideas that are often ignored
in the Shandy world, ideas associated with both Christianity and
empirical observation. Death, for example, can obviously be tied to
final judgment as in the sermon above, but experience also tells us that
death is inevitable for all human flesh. Similarly, human limitations of
knowledge and achievement may be explained by the Fall in Eden, but
again, we can consult our own experience, a lifetime of inevitable gaps
between our satisfactions and our dreams of perfection—our failures
speak for themselves. Insofar as Yorick is clearly identified as a clergyman, it behooves us to consider the possibility that for Sterne—himself
a cleric—he represents not merely empirical observation, but the
Christian view as well.

Yorick's first appearance in *Tristram Shandy* looks in two directions. On the one hand, his actions on behalf of the midwife put him on
Mrs. Shandy's side in the debate over who should "deliver" her; Yorick
will consistently find himself on the women's side in Shandy Hall
because that is always the side of pragmatic observation and action.
Hence, at the Visitation dinner (IV.30.331/394) he has the final word,
an endorsement of "the vulgar" who believe—despite the learned—that
women must play some role in procreation; and at the very end of the
work, it is he who rises up to "batter the whole" of Walter's diatribe
against women "to pieces" (IX.32–33.644–45/804–7).

On the other hand, Sterne introduces Yorick seated upon "a
lean, sorry, jack-ass of a horse, value about one pound fifteen shillings;
who, to shorten all description of him, was full brother to *Rosinante*"
(I.10.18/18). It is important to observe here, and throughout *Tristram
Shandy*, Sterne's reliance upon his reader as a "reader." We have
already seen that Yorick's name entails an awareness of Shakespeare's
Hamlet; now we are told that we are expected to have read Cervantes
also, since *Rosinante* is the name of Don Quixote's horse. However

eccentric or "original" Sterne's book might at first appear, it is a work intricately interwoven with its own literary inheritance; Yorick, in particular, carries the weight of two of Western civilization's greatest literary efforts—and we might add a third when we discover that he keeps a copy of Rabelais in his coat pocket (V.28.387/463).

To say that Yorick is a "quixotic" character might be misleading, however, if only because interpretations of Cervantes's masterpiece are so numerous. It is perhaps safer to say that while Quixote's converting imagination changes his broken-down Rosinante into a magnificent steed, Yorick quite deliberately exchanges a series of splendid mounts for a horse he is literally and metaphorically "riding to death." In a world in which everyone is mounted and galloping upon hobby-horses, a world for which the collision between Obadiah and Dr. Slop (II.9) is a particularly fit emblem, Yorick's choice seems especially telling. I can perhaps risk one more generalization about Sterne's allusion: Cervantes represents for him a mastery of that particular literary irony by which we portray nonsense in a serious tone. This *grave* irony, as Swift—himself a splendid practitioner—labels his own practice,[5] is a benchmark of Augustan satire, a mode of writing that may have been in Sterne's mind in his characterization of Yorick.

For ultimately the portrait of Yorick is a self-justifying portrait of Sterne as a satirist, in part, one suspects, a rewriting of past relations, in part an anticipatory gesture for a *Tristram Shandy* that may or may not have finally emerged. Behind the conversation between Yorick and his cautionary friend, Eugenius, one hears the echo of Pope and his friend, Arbuthnot:

> [A.] 'Good friend forbear! you deal in dang'rous things,
> I'd never name Queens, Ministers, or Kings;
> Keep close to Ears, and those let Asses prick,
> 'Tis nothing'—[P.] Nothing? if they bite and kick?
> Out with it, *Dunciad*! let the secret pass,
> The Secret to each Fool, that he's an Ass. . . .[6]

Yorick, we are told, "had no impression but one, and that was what arose from the nature of the deed spoken of; which impression he

would usually translate into plain *English* without any periphrasis,——
and too oft without much distinction of either personage, time, or
place" (I.11.27/29); and Eugenius warns him that his "unwary pleas-
antry" will sooner or later bring scrapes and difficulties and a hundred
enemies.

The nature of such dialogues between a satirist and friend traces
its heritage back to Horace, another author of importance to keep in
mind during the opening pages of *Tristram Shandy*. Sterne had quoted
him for the motto of his *Political Romance* ("Ridiculum acri / Fortius
et melius magnas plerumque secat Res" ["For ridicule often decides
matters of importance more effectually and forcefully than gravity"])[7];
and Tristram has already asked "Mr. *Horace*'s pardon" for defying his
rules (I.4.8/5). But there is an even more important allusion to Horace
in the *tone* of Sterne's presentation of Yorick, his attempt to capture
the urbane wittiness and cool irony of Horace, a measured and measuring voice that will appear throughout his work as a normative yardstick measuring the intellectual follies and warm enthusiasms
surrounding him.

Here, for example, is a modern translation, delightfully muted in
the Horatian manner, of a few lines from Horace's *Satire, II.3*: "To
delight in building toy houses or hitching up mice / To a cute little cart
or playing "you're it!" or riding / Horsie on a willowy cane would be
sure signs of madness / In a grownup."[8] The genre of satire, particularly among critics trying to rescue Sterne from so "negative" a vision, is
often limited to an angry and devastating literary inheritance, such as
one might associate with Juvenal, another Roman satirist—or with
Swift, in certain moods. Between Horace and Juvenal, however, is a
wide tonal spectrum, within the extremes of which both writers exercise a mode of art that is fundamentally *judgmental* rather than tolerant (tolerance producing comedy, not satire), *discriminating* rather
than *open-minded, institutional* rather than *innovative*. Put this way, it
is evident why many twentieth-century readers *cannot tolerate* the
notion of Sterne as a satirist—or indeed, of satire as a healthy literary
mode. To be *tolerant, open-minded*, and *innovative* are among the
intellectual traits we prize most; writers who do not exhibit such traits
are *excluded* from the pantheon, the doors *closed* against them. This

paradox of modern literary judgment, highlighted by the italicized words in the last two sentences, fascinated Sterne as a universal rather than local phenomenon.[9]

While Tristram declares very early that his motto is *"De gustibus non est disputandum*;—that is, there is no disputing against HOBBY-HORSES" (I.8.13/12), Sterne had written a formal defense of a very different attitude in order to defend his allusion to a real person, Dr. Richard Mead, under the name "Dr. *Kunastrokius*," in the preceding chapter. Mead's private sexual vagaries had been the subject of previous public comment, and Sterne composed a letter to a reader who had—perhaps even prior to publication—objected to his continuing the abuse. Responding to the maxim *de mortuis nil nisi bonum* ("do not speak ill of the dead"), Sterne writes:

> I declare I have considered . . . it over and over again . . . and . . . can find nothing [more] in it . . . than a nonsensical lullaby of some nurse, put into Latin by some pedant, to be chanted by some hypocrite to the end of the world. . . . *"you are not to speak any thing of the dead, but what is good."* Why so?—Who says so?— neither reason or scripture.—Inspired authors have done otherwise—and reason and common sense tell me, that if the characters of past ages and men are to be drawn at all, they are to be drawn like themselves. . . . (*Letters*, 88)

Sterne girds his loins for a battle he never had to fight; if his early intention was to use *Tristram* as a vehicle for the exposure of specific contemporaries, only a few traces remain, the portrait of Dr. Slop and allusions to Bishop Warburton being the most important. Equally significant, however, is his willingness to defend satire against "hypocrites," and to do so on the basis of "reason," "scripture," and "common sense"—sources of judgment marked by their social and political conformity, their celebration of community over individual, since by *reason*, Sterne means "right reason," the eighteenth-century's deceptive term for political power.

As with many satirists, however, the values of an ideal (imaginary) community are used by the individual satirist to measure inadequate communal practice—and here Sterne seems to draw upon his perception of injustices done to his personal ambitions as a clergyman. The portrait of Yorick is filled with contradictions inherent to the satirist's posture. He is a figure of humility, a person who sees himself "in the true point of ridicule," unable to be "angry with others for seeing him in a light, in which he so strongly" sees himself. He is a person of harmony, at one with his horse, able to bring together wit and judgment ("But . . . upon his steed—he could unite and reconcile every thing" [I.10.19–20/20–21]), a problem Tristram will address at length in his "Author's Preface" (III.20). And, finally, he is a person of charity, concerned to save something for the poor, the sick, the afflicted of his parish. In short, he is almost as good a person as Alexander Pope portrays himself to be—as good as we all think ourselves to be, especially in our relations with others.

Yet, the community fails to recognize this. The "temper of the world," we are told, is to ignore Yorick's virtues and pounce on opportunities to accuse him of vice. The sense of personal pain seems strong in Sterne at this juncture, as he points to a better judgment awaiting us than what is available in this life and marks a particular "fatality" in the deeds of "some men": "Order them as they will, they pass thro' a certain medium which so twists and refracts them from their true directions————that, with all the titles to praise which a rectitude of heart can give, the doers of them are nevertheless forced to live and die without it" (I.10.23/24). The cause of this misjudgment, the "medium which so twists and refracts" our capacity to judge others is self-interest; it is Yorick's abuse of that interest that has surrounded him with enemies. There is an attempt to portray these conflicts as the result of accident, of Yorick's gaiety and wit and naïveté, but that misdirection quickly fades when Yorick is confronted with *gravity*. The opposition Sterne posits is not between the "serious" and the "comic"; rather, gravity is affectation, imposition, design, and deceit, whatever opposes or prevents honest judgment. And for this gravity, Yorick has "an invincible dislike and opposition in his nature" (I.11.26/28).

The humility of satirists always collides with their pride, their necessary belief in their capacity to distinguish between good and evil, right and wrong, in order to make precisely the discriminations our century shuns. Yorick is no exception; his attitude is that of the moral absolutist: "*Yorick* had no impression but one, and that was what arose from the nature of the deed spoken of; which impression he would usually translate into plain *English* without any periphrasis." And again: "if it was a dirty action,-----without more ado,-----The man was a dirty fellow" (I.11.27/29). Everything about these sentences goes against recent commentary concerning Sterne; the Shandean world does not appear to be a realm in which *one* impression suffices, in which there can be a redundancy between act and actor, a concurrence translatable into "plain *English.*" It is worth remembering, therefore, that before Sterne reenters Shandy Hall, he will drop a black page across our path, a tribute to Yorick, but also a reminder of the distance between Yorick's world and the world of Sterne's other alter ego, Tristram.

The digressive narrative method of *Tristram Shandy* allows Yorick to reappear *after* his death, and he does so on several occasions. Nowhere is his presence more strongly asserted, however, than in a scene from which he is absent, Trim's reading of the "Abuses of Conscience" sermon to an audience consisting of Walter, Toby, and Dr. Slop. Indeed, the reader is told only after the sermon is read that its author is Yorick:

> I know the author [says Walter], for 'tis wrote, certainly, by the parson of the parish.
> The similitude of the stile and manner of it, with those my father constantly had heard preach'd in his parish-church, was the ground of his conjecture. . . . (II.17.141/165–66)

The parson is, of course, Yorick, and the word *constantly* reminds us of the centrality of the parish-church in the communal life of the eighteenth century. We are also informed that the sermon was preached by a pilfering cleric "at an assize, in the cathedral of *York*, before a thousand witnesses"; Sterne uses the occasion to date Yorick's death, for this fictional cleric not only preached it as his own two years and three months after Yorick's death, but published it as well. Sterne did publish "Abuses of Conscience" some two weeks after he preached it on

29 July 1750, closing the summer assizes. The distance Sterne creates between the Shandy world and the sermon, between the Shandy voices and a Yorick who dies not only in volume I, but again in volume II, his voice and values filtered to us through a fiction of mishap and misappropriation, suggests how difficult it has already become for a normative voice to be heard in the Shandy world.

At the same time, however, the interpolated text calls attention to itself most forcefully, in that there is *no* "distance" between the sermon Sterne preached in 1750 and the one printed in *Tristram Shandy* in 1759—or, for that matter, between these two versions and a second reprinting in volume IV of the collected *Sermons* that Sterne saw through the press in 1766. As with the Sorbonne Memoire in volume I and Ernulphus's Curse in volume III, the verbatim nature of the interpolated material is an important part of its meaning.

That Sterne did not need to alter in any way the sermon he had delivered nine years earlier to a congregation of lawyers and judges provides insight into Yorick's role as the presence of "judgment" in *Tristram Shandy*. Just that stability, that permanence of the Word in relation to the world, is the subject of the sermon; however eager Trim and his auditors (including readers) are to absorb the sermon into the post–black-page Shandy world, it remains what it was: an orthodox Anglican commentary on the relationship between human and divine judgment—particularly suited to an audience whose necessary practice of human justice as members of the judiciary had always to be tempered by their awareness of human fallibility—the abuse of conscience by self-interest. In this regard, satirists and jurists are faced with the same dilemma: how can they judge others, once cognizant of their own fallibility?

"Abuses of Conscience" has a companion piece among Sterne's sermons, "Self-Knowledge"; together the two contain significant borrowings from Swift's two sermons on the same topics: "On the Testimony of Conscience" and "The Difficulty of Knowing One's Self" (published as Swift's work in Sterne's day, but now considered a doubtful attribution). For example, Sterne's opening definition of *conscience* as "the knowledge which the mind has within herself of [our 'thoughts and desires']" (II.17.126/146), seems borrowed from Swift:

"The Word *Conscience* properly signifies, that Knowledge which a Man hath within himself of his own Thoughts and Actions."[10] Swift's language emphasizes the appropriateness of the subject for a juridical audience: "And, because, if a Man judgeth fairly of his own Actions by comparing them with the Law of God, his Mind will either approve or condemn him according as he hath done Good or Evil; therefore this Knowledge or Conscience may properly be called both an Accuser and a Judge" (150).

Sterne, too, extends the legal metaphor, as when he discusses the ways in which the conscience fails: "Could no such thing as favour and affection enter this sacred COURT:—Did WIT disdain to take a bribe in it. . . . Or, lastly, were we assured, that INTEREST stood always uncon-cern'd whilst the cause was hearing,—and that PASSION never got into the judgment-seat, and pronounc'd sentence in the stead of reason, which is supposed always to preside and determine upon the case" (II.17.127/147). But of course "wit" and "interest" and "passion" do interfere with human judgment, whether one is a jurist, a satirist, a philosopher, or, for that matter, a literary critic. The text before us, like our own actions or those of others, is subject to interpretation and the gap between a "dirty action" and a "dirty fellow" may be as nar-row or as wide as we are pleased to make it. Sterne's image of "the lit-tle interests below" that "rise up and perplex the faculties of our upper regions, and encompass them about with clouds and thick darkness" echoes not only Swift's *Tale of a Tub*,[11] where it is perhaps the domi-nant image, but as well "On the Difficulty of Knowing One's Self": "For, as soon as the Appetite is alarmed, and seizeth upon the Heart, a little Cloud gathereth about the Head, and spreadeth a kind of Darkness over the Face of the Soul, whereby it is hindered from take-ing a clear and distinct View of Things" (Swift, *Sermons*, 358).

That such sentiments were expressed in sermons by Anglican ministers might give us pause before we rush to identify assertions of unknowability with modern modes of existential angst and decon-structive indeterminateness. We might especially ask where this view of human weakness takes Swift and Sterne, for the answer will hardly please the modern secularist. Here is Swift's conclusion in "Testimony of Conscience": "It plainly appears, that unless Men are guided by the

Advice and Judgment of a Conscience *founded on Religion*, they can give no Security that they will be either good Subjects, faithful Servants of the Publick, or honest in their mutual Dealings" (Swift, *Sermons*, 158; emphasis mine). Sterne seems to have had Swift before him when composing his own sermon: "So that if you would form a just judgment of what is of infinite importance to you not to be misled in,—— namely, in what degree of real merit you stand either as an honest man, an useful citizen, a faithful subject to your King, or a good servant to your God,–call in religion and morality.—Look,–What is written in the law of God?" (II.17.132/154).

Here is skepticism pressed into the service of religious faith, quite different to be sure from the modern view, which—quite unfairly at times—considers skepticism as religion's antonym. The inability of human beings to judge the world, themselves, or others fairly or accurately, leads clergymen such as Swift and Sterne to an argument for reliance upon a set of received measures and values clustered around the words *God* and *religion*. They did not, to be sure, invent this Christian apology based on skepticism, but could find versions of it in many of their important and favorite predecessors, Montaigne, Erasmus, Pierre Charron, Pascal, Cervantes on the continent, the Latitudinarian divines, especially John Tillotson, in England. Always, whether as Catholic or Protestant apologetics, "skeptical Christianity" arose in response to the perceived dogmatism of the other side—a response to several centuries of increasing Christian sectarian struggle.[12]

One term for this mode of apologetics is *fideism*, although like most religious labels it became subject to sectarian interpretation concerning a possibly excessive reliance on faith. My own emphasis, however, is on fideism's firmly reasoned rejection of unaided human reason in spiritual matters—and hence the need to rely on other resources. Actually, the position might best be defined in relation to opposing polarities. Hence, in the "Abuses of Conscience" sermon Sterne situates himself between the extremes of a Shaftesburian "morality without religion" on the one hand, and Roman Catholic "religion without morality" on the other. The fault of both is *certainty*, whether in the guise of the Earl of Shaftesbury's conviction that we are *infallibly* guided by an innate moral sense that is attracted to the good and eschews the bad, and hence that religion is morally superfluous; or in the Roman Catholic's belief that the darkness surrounding human life is *fully* penetrated by dogma ("All this is impossible with us, quoth Dr. Slop . . . the case could not happen in our Church" [II.17.128–29/149]).

Depending upon his particular argument, Sterne sometimes associates Roman Catholics with Methodists and sometimes with Shaftesbury (freethinkers), a rhetorical gambit he learned from seventeenth-century Anglican polemics, which defended the center against differences that were always defined as extremes and then pretended to see no distinction between the resultant polarities. Sterne's quarrel with Methodists, Roman Catholics, and freethinkers is the same: they pretend to a knowledge that is inaccessible to human beings, to a certainty and absoluteness that belie the unknowingness of the truly religious (and reasonable) posture.

Sterne's position is flawed, much as is the satirist's, in that he is necessarily implicated by the absoluteness he condemns in others. To see this, one need merely observe the religious quarrels of his century as a Jew or Muslim might see them: from this perspective, the centrist position is no more essentially valid or reasonable than the extremes against which it strives to define itself. Swift and Sterne appeal finally to a truth that only faith renders possible, a truth "already written," and revealed to Anglicans as a weapon—like moral absolutes to the satirist—to be turned against those who would dispute the authority of the English ecclesiastical establishment. What is important to understand, however, is Sterne's willing acceptance of that centrist position in his sermon and how its verbatim introduction into *Tristram Shandy* remaps the argument of fideism within a domestic setting.

Sterne's judgment is rarely inquisitorial, he rarely seeks "orthodoxy" or adherence to dogma; rather, he uses his juridical structure as the skeptic does, to demonstrate the inevitable errors of the human mind in relation to the world, and to reveal eccentricities that are wonderfully comic because they resonate with Sterne's sharp ear for the vagaries of language, sexuality, and domestic life. Unlike Swift, whose concerns are more often public and political, Sterne seems deliberately to turn his focus inward. At the same time, however, an inadequate response to the sermon is indeed the "lesson" of the sermon, and as we note the hobby-horsical responses of the Shandy auditors, we come to understand Yorick's continuing presence in the Shandy world, the assertion of communal conscience over individual consciousness.

That Slop falls asleep is a metaphor for what happens to us all when we mount our hobby-horses and enter dreams of order and certainty, explanation and explication. The most deceptive dream of all, the dream at the heart of the sermon, is that we can distinguish (*judge*) correctly between dreaming and waking; that we can, without God's Word and religion and the satirist's reliance upon both, find the line between the innocent and the culpable fictions by which we organize our lives. The scriptural story that most richly embodies both the point of the sermon and the role of the satirist is told in 2 Samuel 12. Here is Sterne's version from the "Abuses of Conscience": "When *David* surprized *Saul* sleeping in the cave, and cut off the skirt of his robe,—we read his heart smote him. . . . But in the matter of *Uriah*, where a faithful and gallant servant . . . fell to make way for his lust . . . his heart smote him not." Sterne notes that a whole year passes between the seduction of Bathsheba and murder of Uriah before Nathan is sent to reprove him, and yet "we read not once of the least sorrow or compunction of heart which he testified, during all that time, for what he had done" (II.17.132/153–54). Nathan tells David the story of a rich man who has killed the lamb of his poor neighbor, and David responds with rage, demanding the name of the malefactor. Nathan's response was well-known to Sterne's audience: "Thou art the man." In this encounter with self-blindness, self-deception, and self-justification one finds the essential core of the satiric spirit, the spirit of Horace and Juvenal, Rabelais and Cervantes, Pope and Swift—and Sterne.

It is a measure of Sterne's control over his writing that the reading of the sermon is halted after its first sentence so that he can introduce a thematic strand that will be picked up toward the end of the sermon—and returned to in the final volume of *Tristram Shandy*—namely, Trim and the Inquisition. Sterne goes to some lengths to concentrate our attention on Trim, devoting several paragraphs before the reading, for example, to a detailed description (in the "grave" manner of Cervantes) of Trim's posture, the "persuasive angle of incidence," sustained by "gravity" in its several senses. When William Hogarth illustrated the scene for Sterne (published as the frontispiece for the second edition) he perceived (or did Sterne suggest it?) that Trim should stand with his back toward the reader; thus, we are in the position of *watching*, rather than *listening to*, Trim. We observe the reading, rather than participate in it. However, as the domestic Shandy audience demonstrates, were we in the original congregation, there would not be a significant difference: *watching* rather than *listening to* the preacher is our first line of defense for keeping our fictions of self-approval intact. The sermon's meaning and presentation coincide.

For Sterne, as both Anglican and skeptic, the Inquisition was a particularly convenient target, an emblem of dogmatism and fanaticism; it had for him a connotation similar to what "gulag" or "concentration camp" might have for us. Opposed to such institutional tyranny is the individual, represented by Trim and his tears, the first significant "sentimental" moment in the work. Sterne's consideration of sentiment may have been triggered by the opening argument of Adam Smith's *Theory of Moral Sentiments*, published in early 1759: "As we have no immediate experience of what other men feel, we can form no idea of the manner in which they are affected, but by conceiving what we ourselves should feel in the like situation." Smith illustrates his point with a scene that resonates with Trim's response to the sermon: "Though our brother is upon the rack, as long as we ourselves are at our ease, our senses will never inform us of what he suffers. They never did, and never can, carry us beyond our own person, and it is by the imagination only that we can form any conception of what are his sensations. . . . By the imagination we place ourselves in his situation, we conceive ourselves enduring all the same torment. . . ." Only when we have done this, have "in some measure" become the "same person with him" can his "agonies . . . begin at last to affect us, and we then tremble and shudder at the thought of what he feels."[13] I discuss sentimentalism more fully in chapter 7, but I quote Smith at length here because Trim's emotional response to the sermon's depiction of the Inquisition seems so clearly to conform to Smith's theory of the origin of sympathy—with one important exception.

In order for his schema to have its moral content, Smith posits that the "brother" is a real person, actually undergoing physical suffering; Sterne, on the other hand, works hard to tell us that Trim is simply imagining an imagining. We cannot validate his identification of the nameless victim as Tom, and indeed would probably want to consider it the same sort of naïve misapprehension of a narrative that Don Quixote experiences watching the puppet show, or Partridge, in *Tom Jones*, watching the performance of *Hamlet*; both comic figures literalize fictions into realities. Trim's naïveté points to the solipsism of Smith's "moral sentiment," his inability to find a starting point for morality other than in the self's capacity to *create* a fiction (an imagining) of suffering. As such, it is a "morality without religion"—the other side of the coin of the Inquisition, which is, obviously, Sterne's "religion without morality."

Trim's response to the sermon, and our willingness to "feel" with him, reenact the moral pitfall that is the subject of the sermon; without reference to authority (God and religion), we cannot or will not distinguish real grief from hobby-horsical grief, our possible sympathy with Tom at the hands of the Inquisition (and our subsequent anger over it—"D—n them all, quoth *Trim*, his colour returning into his face as red as blood" [II.17.138/161–62]) from sympathy with Trim because of his delusion. Bloody wars have been fought under similar delusions mistaken for real griefs, although within the domestic confines of the Shandean household it means only that Mrs. Shandy's real pains of childbirth upstairs are ignored in favor of the imagined pains of Trim, agonizing over the imagined torments of Tom.

It adds considerably to Sterne's irony that his description of the prisoner is a pastiche from other sermon-writers—the levels of fiction separating us from any actual event at this point are indeed multiple. Yorick is not present, however, to educate Trim about the text he is reading; Yorick's death and the black page have announced a brave new world in which Trim and his fellow "readers of the text" will be left to their own "devices and desires," a phrase from the Morning service of the Anglican *Book of Common Prayer*: "Almighty and most merciful Father; We have erred and strayed from thy ways like lost sheep. We have followed too much the devices and desires of our own

hearts." Nor is it Trim and Slop alone who err and stray. We are reading, simultaneously and concomitantly, both the sermon and the book
in which Trim reads the sermon—"we are the ones," as Nathan
reminds us, whose "devices and desires" lead us astray at every turn of
the text. From this perspective, then, the "Abuses of Conscience" is
Yorick's voice from the grave, warning readers of the difficulties of
reading.

It would help our own reading, perhaps, if we leave the moral
(or theological) arena for a moment and focus instead on the implications of the sermon as a guide, not for self-examination, but for its
own interpretation. Can we understand Yorick's sermon? Surely, we
might respond, "if there is any thing in this life" we can depend upon,
it is that we can, as English readers, grasp an "expository" work in
English. Perhaps the Sorbonne *Memoire* might elude us without the
translation in the notes, but for an English reader reading an English
work, it is but to "read ourselves."

Unfortunately, this belief in the easiness of the text will probably
lead us only to Trim's level of response: literal, heartfelt, sincere—and
utterly inaccurate, at least insofar as we may be convinced that the sermon does indeed refer to Tom. Moreover, our own "WIT . . . INTEREST
[and] PASSION" (II.17.127/147) will surely come into play somewhere
in our reading. We probably will want to separate our own sophisti-
cated minds from Trim's simplicity—that is, to demonstrate our *wit*.
We might, if Roman Catholic, rise in defense of our Church, or if
Portuguese, protest the sermon's singling out of that country, or if a
woman, raise the question of Mrs. Shandy's unnoticed screams
upstairs. That is to say, many *interests* will come into play as we read,
not only conscious concerns, but those largely unconscious biases (gender, nationality, religious background) that determine our response to
the world around us—including the text we hold in our hands. And,
finally, *passion*: our need ("desire") to incorporate *Tristram Shandy*
into our own world—to read in such a manner that we master the
work (a male strategy, perhaps) or absorb the work (a female strategy,
perhaps) so that it no longer threatens through its differentness the
constructs by which we have organized the flux and turbulence of life
into coherent and livable patterns.

Moreover, these "biases" are not merely prejudices that we can educate ourselves to avoid; everything in the sermon suggests the opposite, that we must learn to recognize the inevitability of the "biases of the mind," and the danger and destructiveness of our failure to do so. The *self* that reads in the twentieth century has one particular prejudice that *Tristram Shandy* confronts directly and immediately: *"De gustibus non est disputandum"* ("there is no disputing taste"). Relativism, whether in morals or aesthetics, religious preference or social organization, is the cornerstone of the values our intellectual community holds most dear: tolerance, acceptance, openness, broadmindedness. We are, one might suggest, *very prejudiced in favor of toleration*. Moreover, as Nietzsche—that fountainhead of much of modern moral relativism—never tires of pointing out, we cannot escape this paradox. Whether we are the "measure" of the universe is no longer an important question for us; what *is* in our vital interest, however, is to confront Nietzsche's "psychological" observation that we are the world's constant and obsessive "measurers": *"Man as the measurer.* Perhaps all the morality of mankind has its origin in the tremendous inner excitement which seized on primeval men when they discovered measure and measuring, scales and weighing (the word '*Mensch*' [person], indeed, means the measurer, he desired to name himself after his greatest discovery!)" (*Human*, 310). Everywhere in *Tristram Shandy*—and in the critical commentary surrounding it—we observe the paradox: human beings, except in rare, fleeting moments of acute self-consciousness, believe far more than they can ever know, and evaluate their surroundings based on those beliefs in a never-ending process of mismeasurement, misevaluation, and maladjustment.

In a world in which God is the measure, the evasion of this ceaseless human process is faith informed by Grace, a belief in received scripture or religion; in a world in which the human being is the measure, one is left only with the choice of determining whether the mismeasurements are comic or tragic—or possibly both, since we can no longer be certain which is which. To explain why Tristram has torn 10 pages from the book, Sterne emphasizes his moral with the printer's device of an extended index finger: ☞ "A dwarf who brings a standard along with him to measure his own size—take my word, is a dwarf in

more articles than one—And so much for tearing out of chapters"
(IV.25.316/375). Unfortunately, a dwarf is his own "measure," and we
are all dwarfs in this regard, carrying always the inescapable baggage
of our "standards" and "biases," our "tastes" and our "prejudices,"
with us.

Whether one lives in the Shandy world or interprets (reads) it,
what matters is an awareness of our inadequacy and insufficiency,
which cannot be torn from our essential nature like pages from a book.
Yorick dies, abandoning the Shandy world to seeming randomness,
openness, the nonjudgmental, and the infinitely tolerant. But no such
world emerges, neither among the Shandys nor among their readers.
Everyone continues to judge, evaluate, interpret, explain, argue, and
contradict; the rising tide of impotence catches almost everyone, certainly the male Shandys and the critics, Sir and Madam both, for
whom *Tristram Shandy* is always within the grasp of a theory or a
principle. Yorick's death signals not the abandonment of value-making
among the Shandys, but only of the traditional external measure of
those values in Sterne's world, call it Anglicanism, or Grace, or belief
in God and the Word. That Sterne's dazzling chronological game
allows Yorick to reappear in subsequent volumes keeps alive to some
extent that externality. Most important, Yorick feeds our sense of the
comic and tragic futilities of human activity (as he did as a skull in
Shakespeare's *Hamlet*) without the informing presence of essential
(rather than existential) measure. As recent commentators have often
remarked, Shandy Hall is a reflection of many attitudes that constitute
our modern world; it is not, however, a world that Sterne necessarily
endorsed or relished. Zarathustra, that nightmarish Nietzschean voice
of the future, gives us fair warning:

> "And do you tell me, friends, that there is no dispute over taste
> and tasting? But all life is dispute over taste and tasting! Taste:
> that is at the same time weight and scales and weigher; and woe
> to all living creatures that want to live without dispute over
> weight and scales and weigher!" (*Zarathustra*, 140).

6

Heads

Character *Walter*
Foil   *Dr. Slop*
Incident   *The Crushing of Tristram's Nose*
Document   *"Slawkenbergius's Tale"*
Activity   *Knowing*
Image   *The Marbled Page*
-Ism   *Rationalism*

I mistrust all systematizers and avoid them. The will to a system is a
lack of integrity.

(Twilight, 25)

Few characters in literature have been more in love with system-making than Walter Shandy; "he was systematical," says Tristram, "and,
like all systematick reasoners, he would move both heaven and earth,
and twist and torture every thing in nature to support his hypothesis"
(I.19.53/61). Two qualities in general characterize Walter's theories:
first, they all involve power or potency; and second, they all are
undone (rendered impotent) by the actions of the narrative. The sec-

ond point is self-evident: Mrs. Shandy's untimely question, Dr. Slop's forceps, Susannah's inability to remember "Trismegistus," the falling window sash, Walter's failure to make progress on the *Tristrapædia*, all speak to the impotence of his ideas in confrontation with the world.

The first point, however, requires explanation. Walter's initial theory, the necessary concentration of effort in order to ensure the potency of the homunculus is an effort to establish his own role in the procreative process as not merely central but all-encompassing. Let us examine the opening scene, which begins with one of the most famous domestic exchanges in literature: *"Pray, my dear*, quoth my mother, *have you not forgot to wind up the clock?——Good G—!* cried my father, making an exclamation, but taking care to moderate his voice at the same time,*——Did ever woman, since the creation of the world, interrupt a man with such a silly question?"* (I.1.5/2). Critics have often been harsh with Mrs. Shandy (or harsh with Sterne for a perceived "sexist" treatment of her), seeing in her portrayal a marginalized and insignificant woman in a fiction about male relations.[1] I shall return to the women of *Tristram Shandy* in chapter 8, but we might, at this point, distinguish between Sterne's view and Walter's. Walter Shandy considers his wife as colorless, passive, stupid, and unresponsive; she fails, above all else, to acknowledge the potency of those arguments by which Walter intends to shape their world. But to consider anyone through Walter's eyes is to consider the world through the eyes of a foolish person, a point on which Sterne expends considerable labor and wit in the course of his satire. Hence, on our second, if not first, reading of the opening scene, we ought to be alert to the rich ironies of the Shandy bedroom.

Consider, again, the situation: locked in a marital embrace, Walter brings to bear what is left of his sciatica-weakened loins to the task at hand, while Mrs. Shandy, physically beneath him, has—as in that wonderful scene in *Annie Hall*—mentally relocated herself to sit by the side of the bed, observing the scene and thinking of other things to be done on Sunday nights. This is not, I would suggest, her failure of sexual appetite as some critics have opined, but his of performance, and Sterne is shrewd enough to see the relationship between the two almost consistently in that light. By the many clues of Tristram's ille-

gitimacy that hover over the text, abetted by Mrs. Shandy's own unre-
lenting hints in that direction[2]; by her sensible views on midwives versus Walter's dubious reliance on the "scientifick operator," Dr. Slop;
and by her active role in child-rearing versus the never-to-be-ready
Tristrapædia, Sterne seems again and again to trivialize Walter in comparison with Mrs. Shandy. She comes to represent, along with Yorick,
the values and standards by which Sterne *measures* the follies of the
Shandy males.

The initial dialogue tells us something more. Behind Mr. Shandy's
concern with the interruption is his theory of the homunculus, a "phal-
locentric" theory of generation if ever there was one, maintaining that
the entire child in miniature is in the sperm[3] and the woman serves only
to provide a place for gestation. Many of Walter's theories can be dismissed as distinctly ludicrous or purposefully anachronistic, but the
homunculist theory was still credible in the 1760s, although under pres-
sure from the opposing school, the ovulists. What homunculism shares
with Walter's other theories is its diminishment of a woman's role in
the processes of life, a view that culminates in the legal judgment set-
tling the case of the Duke of Suffolk, namely, that "the mother was not
of kin to her child" (IV.29.329/391). Walter is delighted by the intrica-
cies of the argument, but surely its outcome must be equally satisfying,
compatible as it is with his other views. Sterne, on the other hand,
encourages his readers in every possible way to recognize the absurdity
of the legal decision. Toby and Yorick point the way:

> —Let the learned say what they will, there must certainly,
> quoth my uncle *Toby*, have been some sort of consanguinity
> betwixt the duchess of *Suffolk* and her son—
> The vulgar are of the same opinion, quoth *Yorick*, to this hour.
> (IV.30.331/394)

Sterne rejects not simply learning or legalism, but the notion that
the human mind is capable of "rewriting" the world, of giving new
"birth" to it. What might at first glance appear to be a romantic celebration of the natural (the "vulgar") over "book-learning," I read as a
condemnation of that particular mode of moral thought so often asso-

ciated with romantic tendencies, namely, individualism.[4] From this perspective, Sterne is quite opposed to his century's growing faith in the individual's capacity to establish new systems of understanding to replace long-standing communal or received "truths." Faith in the individual mind is the dominant religion of our era, the inheritance of that nineteenth-century romanticism for which Sterne is sometimes—wrongly so, I maintain—considered a major precursor. Put more paradoxically, the Age of Reason was not the eighteenth, but the nineteenth, century, for even the celebration of emotion and spirit that we associate with romanticism pays homage to products of the individual mind (the "heart" and "imagination" being deceptive metaphors for cognitive processes), as I explore further in chapter 7.

The Promethean dream of self-birthing, apparent in many romantic poems and novels, is clearly foreshadowed—but with satiric purpose—in Walter Shandy's procreating by himself, the image manifest in this opening exchange with Mrs. Shandy. It appears again in the decision of the church lawyers that the mother has no kinship with her child. Indeed, it is an idea that finds analogues throughout the work, where separation, isolation, impotence, and finally death everywhere threaten the Shandy males and their celebration of self-sufficiency. No person is more important than Elizabeth Shandy in her embodiment of Sterne's argument against the "singleness" (and "single-mindedness") of the romantic celebration of the individual human mind.

That Walter's chief ally should be a Roman Catholic man-mid-wife, whose "sesquipedality of belly" (II.9.104/121) suggests his own "pregnancy," is further evidence of Sterne's satiric instinct. As noted in chapter 5, Roman Catholicism was readily associated with dogmatism (and error) in the minds of Sterne's largely Protestant audience. Moreover, invoking Rabelais, Montaigne, and Swift as his primary Muses, Sterne could associate with their skepticism, their opting always for a contradiction of any positive assertion of human reason. It has almost always been the arrogance of science that elicits the satiric argument against it, rather than any inherent aspect of the scientific method. Indeed, the anatomical pragmatism of science often finds a quite parallel spirit in satire. It is not Slop's science, but his certainty that evokes Sterne's ridicule.

Sterne enriches his portrayal of Slop by a second satiric method, reference to a known personality. Dr. Richard Burton, his fellow Yorkshireman and man-midwife had published in 1751 his magnum opus of scientific progress, an *Essay towards a Complete New System of Midwifry*, a work that was quite upstaged a year later by William Smellie (Sterne's satire has, at times, difficulty keeping up with real life!), whose *Treatise on the Theory and Practice of Midwifery* was much more favorably received. Following the typical eighteenth-century practice, Burton did what all scholars of his day would have done—he riposted in a 250-page *Letter to William Smellie, M.D., Containing Critical and Practical Remarks upon his Treatise*. The discussion at the end of volume II concerning childbirth is copied directly from this counterblast.

If we look more closely at the title of Burton's first work, we may note an interesting contradiction. On the one hand, it is an *essay towards*, suggesting a tentativeness with ideas that Sterne would consider proper for all human endeavor. But three other words, *complete*, *new*, and *system*, contradict that tentativeness and in them we can locate much of Sterne's satire on Dr. Slop, on Walter Shandy, and on the "modern" age they adumbrate. Let me first observe that the obstetrical advances of the eighteenth century, particularly in substituting trained physicians for midwives, had a great deal to do with the century's dramatic decline of fatalities (mother or child) in the birthing process. A simpleminded attack against science, and especially against science as a male preserve (it was so only because of a closed educational system), may serve some political agenda, but hardly seems fair when produced on a word processor rather than with a quill. On the other hand, what characterizes Smellie's obstetrics as opposed to Burton's is his interest in "cooperating" with the natural process and the truly "scientific" tentativeness of his conclusions.

Sterne's eye for this difference between the two "scientists" was acute. For example, Burton only once mentions the desirability of podalic (feet first) delivery, but Sterne pounces on his statement, making it central to his own presentation of Slop. Similarly, the suggestion of cesarean section, at which Mrs. Shandy pales with good reason (since the first such operation in which the mother survived was not until 1793), is mentioned by Burton but hardly anyone else in the century. But above all, it is Burton's blind and total faith in instruments, particularly his own forceps, that plays into Sterne's satiric hand. What hovers over and unites all these suggestions is the presence of abortion and death, the birthing (creative) process gone awry. When the head does not present first, every effort is made to turn the child, because a feet-first delivery is extremely dangerous to both child and mother; a cesarean operation in the eighteenth century was used primarily to extract a child from a dead mother; and the instruments in Slop's bag are not instruments of "deliverance," but of death, tools by which to destroy and extract fetuses when all hope of a live birth is lost.[5] Only the forceps might have had a more hopeful use, but of course in Slop's hands they too are a symbolic instrument of death, crushing the Shandy family's hope for a good, jolly nose for Tristram.

Sterne's very conscious melding of ideas of birth and death in the opening volumes of *Tristram Shandy*, volumes that concentrate on Walter's systems and theories, serves not merely as a metaphor for the processes of human understanding (creation = procreation), but as a measure of them as well. Slop believes the salvation of the Shandy line rests on his invention of the forceps; Walter rests his new hope for the line on the theory of "auxiliary verbs," an "instrument" for drawing out of the child's brain "a magazine of conceptions and conclusions" (V.43.406/486). But of course the theory, although drawn from an actual educational manual of the seventeenth century, Obadiah Walker's *Of Education* (1673), is inane—as with all good satirists, Sterne's forte is finding the ridiculous in serious human efforts, rather than in his own inventions. The theory is a process of sterile vocalization, producing dead ideas that take us back to the discussion in volume II about the location of the soul and the capacity to live without a brain. Walter's "north-west passage" is a means of living without thinking, living by words, but divorced from the community that gives language its boundaries (that is, its definitions). Put another way, the theory of auxiliary verbs is a profound step toward solipsism, the independence of the self from "*common* sense," that community of agreement by which readers for two centuries have shared the awareness that the discussion generated about the "white bear" is "*non*-sense."

The notion of "*common* sense" is a dangerous one, replete with social and political implications, since community is the tyranny of the majority—or, equally possible, the minority with the most power. That danger, however, should not blind us to the meaningfulness of the notion to Sterne—and to every society. Much of Sterne's creative energy goes toward his effort to preserve the validity of communal thought against the challenges of rising individualism; like Pope, Swift, and Samuel Johnson, to name other authors obsessed with the same question, Sterne consistently seeks the means by which human assertions could be weighed and measured. Behind the humor of Walter's inadequate systems lies a testing of the entire spectrum of human knowledge, from revealed truth at one end to Dryden's "*nonsense* absolute"[6] at the other. In between, are the playing fields of human endeavor.

Nowhere is this exploration of the human way with ideas more humorously portrayed than in "Slawkenbergius's Tale," which, as Walter's favorite story in his favorite book, may be taken as a paradigm for his character. To begin to understand this "document," we might turn to the very beginning of *Tristram Shandy*, the motto to volumes I and II. The sentence comes originally from Epictetus, but probably reached Sterne via one of his favorite books, Montaigne's *Essays*; Charles Cotton renders the sentence thus: "MEN (says an ancient *Greek* Sentence) are tormented with the Opinions they have of Things, and not by the Things themselves." This reflects the "life and opinions" of the title, but one astute reader, Donald Greene, has suggested that we look more closely at the Greek original, since that is what Sterne actually offers us on his title page. Greene's transliteration into the Roman alphabet and his interlinear translation cast interesting new light:

> Ou ta Pragmata tarassei tous Anthrōpous,
> Not practicalities trouble human beings,
> alla ta Dogmata peri tōn Pragmatōn.
> but dogmas concerning practicalities.

Greene concludes: "It seems to me that the epigraph will be closer to what Sterne wanted us to read if we give it a more modern rendering:

what is needed is pragmatism, not dogmatism; it is not reality that causes most trouble for the human race but far-fetched, thin-spun, rigidly held theories imposed on reality by pride in the human capacity for ratiocination."[7] With this dichotomy, pragmatism versus dogmatism, firmly in mind let us examine "Slawkenbergius's Tale."

We should remember first that the episode concludes a lengthy discussion about noses, really a discussion about penises and sexual potency. As such, it is a piece with Walter's and Slop's interest in both masculine self-sufficiency and power. Slop is, of course, the "bridge"; having had his nose crushed by the forceps, Tristram must now tell us why this was a crushing blow to his father's hopes—an explanation that entails Walter's theory of Noses. Tristram proceeds with blatant misdirection: "For by the word *Nose*, throughout all this long chapter of noses, and in every other part of my work, where the word *Nose* occurs,—I declare, by that word I mean a Nose, and nothing more, or less" (III.31.218/258). His leaky tautology is embodied in Don Diego, whose silence concerning his journey to the "Promontory of Noses" is in stark contrast to the noise of interpretation surrounding him. Interpretation is necessary, however, since the assertion of an identity (nose = nose) that would render discussion superfluous, is clearly a deception: nose no longer means nose within the Shandy discourse.

As readers, interpreters of the text, we are seduced into contributing to that noise—indeed, the Strasburgers' attempt to read Diego parallels our own attempt to read *Tristram Shandy*. "Slawkenbergius's Tale" is perhaps best understood as a lesson in how to read—or, better, how we *do* read, and how best to correct certain dangerous predilections. As such, it has a marked similarity to the "Abuses of Conscience" sermon.

· The "Tale" is prefaced by the marbled page with its invitation to penetrate its moral ("motly emblem of my work"); and by a discussion of the excesses of "verbal criticism." The progression from the black page representing death, to a marbled page (no two of which are alike and all of which had to be produced individually by hand) representing, perhaps, the complexities of interpretation, of knowing anything, may suggest a shift from Yorick's world to Walter's (or Tristram's), from the certainty of death to the uncertainty of everything else.

Equally possible, however, it represents the return of Yorick (associated as he is with the first emblematic page) to the scene, for the uncertainty of things (the chances and changes of the world, which are integral to the process of marbling) is Yorick's vision far more than Walter's, whose instinct is to "fix" whatever is in flux, to control accident and chance by the capacity of his mind to create systems of order and arrangement. Significantly, given the imagery of male potency underscoring the entire discussion, we are invited to "penetrate" the marbled page, which thus becomes, in turn, in its highly resistant unresponsiveness to systems of order, an emblem of Mrs. Shandy, of the feminine life that Walter and Slop, and now Tristram and Slawkenbergius, will try to master through exclusion. The diffusion of colors might also suggest the diffusion of Walter's sperm in the opening scene; the chances and changes that mark life defy penetration, and the celebration of male potency is clouded before it begins.

Most important, the various physical failures that emerge in the Shandy world are never contained, but ramify continually as mental aberrations—as the theories, explanations, and interpretations of a hobby-horsical world. Walter as a procreative father is a dubious figure at best; but after the opening scene we see him as the progenitor not of sons but of ideas, a pedant armed with certainty and a penknife (another phallic representation, surely). Reinforcing the implications of the marbled page, the chapter following (III.37) shows us Walter Shandy as a reader of the text, in this instance, Erasmus's *Familiar Colloquies*: "Nature had been prodigal in her gifts to my father beyond measure, and had sown the seeds of verbal criticism . . . deep within him . . . so that he had got out his penknife . . . to see if he could not scratch some better sense into it.—I've got within a single letter . . . of *Erasmus* his mystic meaning. . . . See . . . how I have mended the sense.—But you have marr'd a word, replied my uncle *Toby*" (III.37.230/272). Walter here joins such important satiric figures of the eighteenth century as Peter in Swift's *Tale of a Tub*, who, as an embodiment of Roman Catholicism's abuse of Scripture (in Anglican eyes), is able to find whatever he wants in his text; and Lewis Theobald, an editor of classical texts, and Pope's first choice as the chief dunce of his *Dunciad*. What all three targets share is the imposition of their egos on texts that are clearly considered to exist independent of both readers and reading. It is a measure of the integrity with which Swift, Pope, and Sterne want to endow the Word (and, hence, all words) that violators are held among the highest objects of ridicule.

That Sterne is undertaking an examination of questions similar to those explored in the *Tale* and the *Dunciad*, questions concerning the validation of revelation (religious truth) and inspiration (poetic excellence), is made clear in the next chapter, especially in Sterne's introduction to Slawkenbergius's "grand FOLIO":

> Tell me . . . what secret impulse was it? what intonation of voice? whence came it? how did it sound in thy ears?—art thou sure thou heard'st it?—which first cried out to thee [to write his great work]. . . .
>
> How the communication was conveyed into *Slawkenbergius*'s sensorium,——so that *Slawkenbergius* should know whose finger touch'd the key,——and whose hand it was that blew the bellows . . . we can only raise conjectures.
>
> *Slawkenbergius* was play'd upon, for aught I know, like one of *Whitfield*'s disciples,——that is, with such a distinct intelligence, Sir, of which of the two *masters* it was, that had been practising upon his *instrument*,——as to make all reasoning upon it needless. (III.38.230–31/272–73)

The sudden appearance of the name of George Whitefield (1714–70), the great Methodist preacher, is only one clue of several that Sterne's ultimate context is religious enthusiasm and its concomitant concerns, visitation and authentication. In the seventeenth century, the Anglican church felt compelled to argue that individual revelations claimed by Protestant dissenters were the result of zeal and self-delusion. In his sermons of the mid-eighteenth century, Sterne directed these earlier arguments against similar Methodist claims of personal visitation. Here in *Tristram Shandy*, he uses the same anti-"enthusiast" language to surround Slawkenbergius—and Walter Shandy—with the implications of misguided (Methodist) zeal. The image of the organ ("finger touch'd the key . . . hand . . . blew the bellows") is pregnant with imagery usually surrounding polemic discussions of false inspiration;

and the mention of the two *"masters"* approaches the fundamental question regarding claims of visitation, whether the inspiring "wind" is divine or demonic?

Moreover, Slawkenbergius's justification for writing is suspiciously pious; ever since he arrived at the age of discernment and was able "to sit down coolly, and consider within himself the true state and condition of man, and distinguish the main end and design of his being . . . [he has] felt a strong impulse, with a mighty and an unresistible call within . . . to gird [himself] up" to this undertaking" (III.38.231/ 273–74). Sterne opens his sermon "Trust in God" with this sentence: "WHOEVER seriously reflects upon the state and condition of man" and toward the end comments on "whoever cooly sits down and reflects upon the many accidents . . . which have befallen him" (*Sermons* [1769], VI:3, 24); in both instances the result is a belief in a providential God, not the production of a new text but the endorsement of an old. Further, the "girding" of oneself is a biblical commonplace, as, for example, in this particularly apropos verse: "Thou therefore gird up thy loins, and arise, and speak unto them all that I command thee"— the voice of God to one of the *inspired* prophets (Jeremiah 1:17).

As a writer, Slawkenbergius is the archetypal scholastic philosopher, a point Sterne makes by telling us his book "may properly be considered, not only as a model,—but as a thorough-stitch'd DIGEST and regular institute of *noses*; comprehending in it, all that is, or can be needful to be known about them" (III.38.232/274). The idea of an "institute" is one of Sterne's favorites: he describes Ernulphus's curse as an "institute of swearing" (III.12.183/215), and the *Tristrapædia*, which he sits "down coolly" to write, in a similar manner (V.16.372/ 445). One might also recall Dr. Burton's "complete new system" of midwifery. The Scriblerian suggestion that the gathering of *all* available information will result in *systems* of perfect knowledge is as ludicrous to Sterne in the 1760s as it was to Pope and Swift a generation earlier.

This context of scholasticism and textual study prepares us for the digression that follows, the quarrel between Prignitz and Scroderus, who anticipate in their debate (whether fancy begets the nose, or the nose begets the fancy) the debate of the Strasbourg logicians, whether the man belongs to the nose or the nose to the man; in both instances, Sterne parodies philosophy's long interest in efficient and accidental causes, substances and attributes, and other Aristotelian subjects to which he gave little credence. Walter resolves the debate by alluding to material lifted from Rabelais (on Ambrose Paré), another clue to the scholastic context of the discussion; and Sterne's style at this point imitates Rabelais's (and Swift's) noisy redundancy and excess of language madly pursuing truth: "his nose was so snubb'd, so rebuff'd, so rebated, and so refrigerated" and "the nose was comforted, nourish'd, plump'd up, refresh'd, refocillated, and set a growing for ever" (III.38.234/277). Tristram calls attention in the next paragraph to the "utmost chastity and decorum of expression" used by Paré since he is focused (and wants us to focus) on Paré's bawdy possibilities; Sterne, I suspect, would like us to admire, instead, the exuberant fecundity of a style that offers—as in Rabelais and Swift—so devastating a contrast to the emptiness of its content, the futility of its attempt to systematize the richness of experience. Equally important, the argument of Ambrose Paré overthrows "the peace and harmony" of the Shandy family. We are never told why this happens, because Tristram runs out of time; this pattern of debate and disturbance, however, will be repeated in the "Tale" itself.

That Walter's imagination is "heated" by "long noses" (III.39.236/279) we can, by this time, readily understand; he is, like Slawkenbergius, an enthusiast; what remains is that he proselytize: "nothing would serve him but to heat my uncle *Toby*'s [imagination] too." Lighting the "*damp* tinder" of Toby's brain is, however, no easy task, not even for the "warmer paroxisms of [Walter's] zeal"; one might sense here an analogy to the opening scene where Walter's attempt to impregnate Mrs. Shandy meets with a similar "dampening." There the dialogue ended with the significant word, "Nothing"; here the clash of ideas brings one to the silence of faith: "Let humble gratitude acknowledge the effect, unprompted by an idle curiosity to explain the cause" is the way Sterne states it in his sermon, "On Enthusiasm" (*Sermons* [1769], VI:140). Toby's "solution" to the problem of long noses is a comic restatement of the same principle: "God pleases to have it so" (III.41.240/284), he argues. That Walter recognizes the source of this argument in Rabelais ("That is *Grangousier*'s solution, said my father"), reinforces its roots in the tradition of Christian skepticism, a tradition that posits (not fairly, to be sure) the radical simplicity of Christian truth and hence a skeptical response to all other systems of belief and knowledge. Like Sterne, Toby allows the titans of ideas to clash above his head, while the business of life is pursued elsewhere. *Tristram Shandy*—and its longest interpolated episode, "Slawkenbergius's Tale"—might well be considered words to accompany Toby's musical response to Walter's "idle curiosity," a more than usually *zealous* whistling of Lillabullero (III.41.241/285).

Sterne chose Strasbourg not only because of its untimely "demise" at the hands of Lewis XIV, but even more because it was a city he could neatly divide between Lutherans and Roman Catholics— Strasbourg was, geographically and theologically, an important Protestant thrust into Catholic France. This context might suggest a prophetic or apostolic moment when Diego alights for his walk around town and dons his crimson-satin breeches with the silver-fringed cod-piece, Sterne's comic translation of the Greek *Perizomate*, a girdle worn round the loins and appearing in such scriptural phrases as "Thou therefore gird up thy loins, and arise, and speak unto them all that I command thee" (Jeremiah 1:17).

But Diego speaks very little and rather than prophesying to or proselytizing the people, he makes it a point of honor to refuse them any "conviction" concerning the *truth* of his nose; and his quick departure prevents the main disputants from seeing him (as do the townspeople) or overhearing his several conversations on the road (as do the readers). Yet those who do see require "touch" for certainty; and those who overhear are more interested in what is *unsaid* than said. The incomplete sentence or word is Diego's most characteristic style—*climaxing*, one might suggest, in Julia's lament that she will die "*un*——" (IV.S.T.269/321). Despite the editors of the Florida edition, who believe *undone* would best complete the sentence, Diego's offering of "*unconvinced*" ought not be dismissed. Much in the "Tale" revolves around the problem of *conviction* in its peculiarly Anglican guise, the question of faith and validation. Diego's journey is designed to produce a *conviction* of potency in Julia; its result is, instead, an obsessive search for *conviction* among the Strasbourgers, and a loss of their potency as they lose their town to a French invasion.

The attempt to understand, to "read," Diego parallels Walter's way with Erasmus's text and more generally with the world. But having described the sleeplessness of the female church dignitaries and the "restlessness and disquietude" of the males (the sexual allusions weave a web of erotic curiosity around our need for knowledge, and tie the "Tale" closely to the play of impotence in the Shandy bedroom), Sterne offers another parallel: "such a zealous inquiry into the cause of that restlessness, had never happened in *Strasburg*, since *Martin Luther*, with his doctrines, had turned the city up-side down" (IV.S.T.255/303). By reconstructing the historical Strasbourg and allowing it to speak for itself, Sterne seems to reduce all religion to noisy debate and dichotomy. However, the center of power and belief, Don Diego, remains untouched by these quarrels and divisions, not merely silent or aloof, but absent. He is, we might say, the center of attention but not of the discourse—and, indeed, if we listen carefully to that discourse, we come to realize how Swiftian, how satiric, Sterne can be in deploring what the human mind does with its gifts. There is much celebration of the "democracy of minds" among modern readers of Sterne, but it is difficult to see anything but rejection and repudiation in his handling of "the riot and disorder" of the city and the futility of the learned, who argue "so many strange things, with equal confidence on all sides, and with equal eloquence in all places" (IV.S.T.255/303). Sterne listens very carefully to the noise of the human discourse, which produces his capacity to parody it with great brilliance. But parody is not approval.

Strasbourg is turned into the England of a century earlier, when an advocate of the "truth" preached on every street corner to the ready ears of the populace. The most popular is the "trumpeter's wife," who stands "upon a stool in the middle of the great parade"— "But when a demonstrator in philosophy (cries *Slawkenbergius*) has a *trumpet* for an apparatus, pray what rival in science can pretend to be heard besides him" (IV.S.T.257/305). The medical faculty, the logicians, the lawyers, all have their say on the matter, but their wildly different discussions all share a common device: whatever one side opines, the other side offers a counteropinion.

What attracts Sterne is clearly not the substance of any one argument, but rather its calling forth a counterargument:

> He dies of a plethora, said they . . .
> It happens otherways—replied the opponents.——
> It ought not, said they. (IV.S.T.258–59/308)

or:

> Now death, continued the logician, being nothing but the stagnation of the blood—
> I deny the definition—Death is the separation of the soul from the body, said his antagonist—Then we don't agree about our weapon, said the logician—Then there is an end of the dispute, replied the antagonist. (IV.S.T.259/309)

Despite the "scientific" content of these exchanges, their model is clearly theological scholasticism, and we are not surprised when the ecclesiastic court underwrites its first decision with a footnote of legalistic gibberish; as D. W. Jefferson noted long ago, the satire of learned wit considers the various faculties (law, medicine, literature) and the church as interchangeable targets.[8]

Why does Sterne revive an argument against a mode of thinking clearly passé in mid-eighteenth-century England? One strong clue is provided by the literary antecedents of Walter Shandy in the *philosophus gloriosus* figure of classical comedy. Sterne's favorite encyclopedist, Ephraim Chambers defines scholasticism as a school "wholly taken up in frivolous questions" debated "with great heat," and "now fallen into the last contempt," but the "scholastic" way of the human being with ideas certainly preceded medieval Christianity—and outlasted it as well. It was alive among the Greek philosophers and the Jewish rabbis before the birth of Jesus, and continued in Sterne's day, long after the heyday of the church schoolmen, in those numerous, perhaps infinite challenges to established thought that marks the argument and counterargument of human discourse. One can discuss particular modes of counterargument, the Methodists, for example, with their positiveness concerning individual revelation, or the new scientists, equally positive that they had discovered, with Walter, the northwest passage to truth, but the essential problem is to locate Sterne amidst this pull and tug of ideas. His career within the Anglican establishment offers a clue worth pursuing, if only because it counters the modern tendency to deny the centrality of communal religion in any intellectual construct.

Sterne, I maintain, defined his own intellectual pursuits within that framework, as did many—if not all—of the great thinkers of his age, including John Locke and Isaac Newton. Hence, with the simple (simplistic?) division of all theological questions into two camps, the one "practical," the other "polemical," Sterne could dismiss as beside the point all "counterarguments" to the communal positions with which he identified: "The stranger's nose was no more heard of in the dispute—it just served as a frigate to launch them into the gulph of school-divinity" (IV.S.T.264/315). When we note that Chambers considers the term *school-divinity* a synonym for scholasticism, we begin to understand how Sterne's position evolves. Toward the end of the volume that opens with the "Tale" Sterne delivers an opinion concerning the correct mode of preaching that is deceptively complex in its embrace of simplicity: "To preach, to shew the extent of our reading, or the subtleties of our wit . . . but convey little light and less warmth—is a dishonest use of the poor single half hour in a week which is put into our hands—'Tis not preaching the gospel—but ourselves—For my own part, continued *Yorick*, I had rather direct five words point blank to the heart—" (IV.26.317/377). A year later, in volume V, Sterne devotes a full chapter (chapter 29) to quoting a ludicrous passage from Rabelais (Gymnast's acrobatic feats on his horse) because Yorick considers it an apt description of "polemic divines": "I wish there was not a polemic divine, said *Yorick*, in the kingdom;—one ounce of practical divinity—is worth a painted ship load of all their reverences have imported these fifty years" (V.28.387/462).

Connected to this dismissal of polemical divinity is Sterne's condemnation of the sectarian nature of intellectual debate, the immediate

division into Nosarian and Antinosarian sides and then, as the parish-
ioners are inflamed and "left in all the distresses of desire unsatisfied,"
the further divisions into *Parchmentarians*, *Brassarians*, and
Turpentarians (IV.S.T.264/315). Had Sterne consulted Chambers's
Cyclopedia under *Lutheranism*, he would have found 39 different sects
listed, including the Samosatenses, Inferani, Antidiaphorists, and
Antiswenkfeldians. The world of position and counterposition opens
us to never-ending division and divisiveness. The warfare of dogma, of
system, of ideology, is, indeed, the history of the world.

Sterne points us to one additional "moral" of the "Tale" with
two of those wonderfully abrupt and pointed sentences which so often
punctuate the seemingly undisciplined "drift" of his narrative style.
The first is a commonplace yet devastating aphorism: "Heat is in pro-
portion to the want of true knowledge" (IV.S.T.264/315). The second
sentence occurs at the climax of the "Tale," where Slawkenbergius
himself locates the end of the "Catastasis": "——The poor Strasburgers left upon the beach!" (IV.S.T.264/315; cf. 266/317). As a guardian
of the Anglican establishment, Sterne saw zeal and dogmatism ("Little
boots it to the subtle speculatist to stand single in his opinions"
[I.19.55/63]) as public dangers. But while Swift, his historical horizon
bounded by the Interregnum, feared most the manipulation of the
mob, the proselytizing of the "vulgar" by devious and insane enthusiasts, Sterne's attitude is more relaxed. A comic and tragic futility is
found in the human desire for certainty and conviction, and somewhere among Rabelais, Montaigne, Burton, Locke, Chambers, and
Swift, Sterne sought a skeptical stance that would deny the absolutism
of dogmatists while preserving his own (and his congregation's) capacity to believe in the concept of Truth. Sterne could not abandon his
own certainty concerning Anglican centrism; hence, his blindness to
the rhetorical gambits and dogmatics of his own argument that one
need only "preach the gospel" or direct words "to the heart." This lat-
ter approach, a particularly significant strategy for Sterne and his age,
will be examined in the next chapter, but surely we can agree that in
both instances, Sterne pretends to a simplicity of interpretation and
reception that is nonexistent. The gospel is never self-evident, and the

heart (a blood pump) is never free, except metaphorically, from the weaknesses and biases of the body and mind.

In order to protect his congregation from the errors of zeal, Sterne invests "moderation" and "silence" with considerable power, while heaping enervating ridicule on language and system and rationalism. The discrepancy between the potency of Don Diego and Walter's impotence (and Tristram's flattened nose) is the vehicle of his satire on the pretensions of human reason when measured against a system he accepted as revealed and originary rather than human and rational. Significantly, the "Tale" is framed by images of "Truth." Before it begins, Tristram draws on Locke's *Essay Concerning Human Understanding*, to define the "great and principal act of ratiocination in man" as the "finding out the agreement or disagreement of two ideas one with another, by the intervention of a third; (called the *medius terminus* [the middle term]) just as a man, as *Locke* well observes, by a yard, finds two mens nine-pin-alleys to be of the same length, which could not be brought together, to measure their equality, by *juxtaposition*" (III.40.237/280–81). And at the conclusion of the "Tale," Slawkenbergius dismisses the various theories concerning the demise of Strasbourg in this manner: "It is the lot of few to trace out the true springs of this and such like revolutions—The vulgar look too high for them—Statesmen look too low—Truth (for once) lies in the middle" (IV.S.T.271/323). Sterne alters Locke's "two Houses" to "two mens nine-pin-alleys," setting up a rather perverse possibility because of "yard," an eighteenth-century term for *penis*. Similarly, his parenthetical "for once" in the second statement suggests an ironic recognition on Sterne's part of the difficulty of his own position, the infinite regression of conflicting systems to a "truth" that is neither present nor articulated; like Don Diego, truth leaves only its trace behind, a mystery that invites rather than inhibits debate. Sterne grasped full well the irony of a faith that had to be embodied in the potencies of absence and silence. Still, the impotent surrender of the Strasbourgers to the "grand system of Universal Monarchy" (triumphant dogmatism?), and, indeed, the impotence that hovers everywhere over the Shandy world, makes Don Diego a force to be reckoned with. Whether he represents the "power of love" as Julia would find him; or the "state of rest and quietness" to which Slawkenbergius, seeing the world as a stage, finally brings his hero, we need not determine: an Anglican clergyman would be at home with either text—"the peace of God, which passeth all understanding" (Philippians 4:7).

Walter Shandy is, above all else, a believer in language, in the power of human beings to shape the truth of their world with words. This is evident in his theory of names, for example, his strong belief in the magic of naming being a paradigm for the enterprise of science: to provide a name is to give identity, substance, quality, to what seems to be unknown without one. Walter's faith in words is also evident in his theory of auxiliary verbs, a triumph of the mechanical operation of the spirit in restless pursuit of words that might better arrange one's relationship with the unknown and unfamiliar. But it is Walter's theory of noses that most clearly suggests Sterne's understanding of the crucial dependency between world and word, between power and knowledge.

Most important is the fundamentally flawed tautology in the definition alluded to earlier, for nose definitely does not mean nose within Walter's world. This slippage in definition does not mean, however, as some modern commentators have argued, that Sterne perceives an infinitely free play, a randomness that coincides with modern theories of the indeterminacies of language. Indeed, quite the opposite happens, and Sterne's insight may be shrewder than our own. The gap that opens within the tautology, the distance between "nose" and "nose," is comic, but not innocent; and the ease with which "nose" (and indeed all oblong shapes in *Tristram Shandy*) is converted into penis for *every* reader signals the dangers of what George Orwell, in *1984*, would call *Newspeak*. That is to say, Walter and Tristram together impose their own idea of order on the reader, and we are quite unable to resist. Every shape, every nook and cranny, every line and every circle, becomes pregnant with meaning, and the word *pregnant*, as I just used it, is itself *implicated*—as is *implicated*, the Latin root of which means to "fold into." The susceptibility of language to constant change and imposition is part of Sterne's interest in Walter Shandy, and the benignity of the humorous portrayal is everywhere challenged by the inescapability of his underlying premise: in the gap between word and world there may be room for play, but there is also tremendous opportunity for demagoguery and disaster. In the Shandy world, Walter, the demagogue of language, does not have the cannons; and Toby, whose being is defined by cannons, does not have language. When, however, language and cannons come together, as they have so often in the history of the human race, the gap between word and world is the fertile ground on which black can be turned into white, nose into penis, good into evil. It is also a world in which Sterne's silent core of truth, a "simple" religion that speaks itself, is overwhelmed by the noise of conflicting systems and theories and perhaps disappears completely.

Nietzsche's high praise of Sterne has much to do, I believe, with Sterne's insight that the collapse of identity between word and world might not turn out to be the happy holiday suggested by those caught up in notions of liberation and new knowledge. I quote from an early section of *Human, All Too Human*: *"Language as putative science—*. . . . To the extent that man has for long ages believed in the concepts and names of things as in *aeternae veritates* . . . he really thought that in language he possessed knowledge of the world. . . . A great deal later— only now—it dawns on men that in their belief in language they have propagated a tremendous error" (*Human*, 16). Language and logic depend on presuppositions with which "nothing in the real world corresponds," for example "on the presupposition that there are identical things, that the same thing is identical at different points of time . . ." (16).[9] Nietzsche's ideal philosopher-king, his Zarathustra, can live with this knowledge, because Zarathustra knows how to remain infinitely flexible and uncommitted, hovering among all possibilities as classical skepticism instructs us to do. But the terrible pains inherent in this lack of position, the human inability to resist succumbing to the dreams of order that surround us, is perhaps Nietzsche's dominant subject. His most dire warnings (prophecies) are not concerned so much with the disappearance of Truth in the modern world, as with his insistence that Truth will never be found by certain people: "Do not be jealous, lover of truth, because of these inflexible and oppressive men! Truth has never yet clung to the arm of an inflexible man" (*Zarathustra*, 79). That the twentieth century produced major villains of inflexibility, one of whom linked his totalitarian system to

Nietzsche's philosophy, is a cruel irony that neither Nietzsche nor Sterne would shrink from understanding; the fundamental question for both was never epistemological (How can we know the truth?), but moral (How is it possible to live without the truth?). The nature of one's beliefs, one's truths, is the overwhelming issue, and the primary reason why Sterne could not end *Tristram Shandy* with the dismemberment of Walter Shandy. With Walter's dance of the white bear at the end of volume V, his dominance of *Tristram Shandy* comes to an end; volumes VI, VIII, and IX will concentrate on the alternative offered by Toby Shandy, the subject of the next chapter.

7

Hearts

Character	*Toby*
Foil	*Trim*
Incident	*The Courting of Widow Wadman*
Document	*Toby's Apologetical Oration*
Activity	*Feeling*
Image	*Trim's Flourish with his Stick*
-Ism	*Sentimentalism*

I understood the ever spreading morality of pity that had seized even on philosophers and made them ill, as the most sinister symptom of a European culture that had itself become sinister.[1]

In 1967, John Traugott, whose study of Sterne's "philosophical rhetoric" in 1954 had already become the dominant critical approach to *Tristram Shandy*,[2] gathered a collection of essays on Sterne designed primarily for undergraduates who could not be expected to use library resources as would scholars and graduate students. In its introduction he wrote a few *simple* declarative sentences on Uncle Toby, dogmatic statements not only in keeping with what I have elsewhere labeled his existential-sentimental approach to *Tristram*, but closed to debate from his perspective: "War is a stock subject of moralists," he wrote, but "all this is irrelevant to Sterne. What is relevant is Toby's bowling-green war, a private fantasy. . . . Is Toby really blood-thirsty? The question is irrelevant."[3]

Traugott's collection appeared in 1968, the bicentenary anniversary of Sterne's death, which was celebrated in Coxwold during the week of the Democratic Party convention in Chicago, where protesters against the Vietnam Conflict were clubbed in the streets. It was as well, and perhaps not coincidentally, the year French and American campuses exploded over the question of whether *anything* in the university curriculum was "relevant" in light of the "warmongering," "blood-thirsty" establishment under attack. That Traugott was teaching at the University of California, Berkeley—the scene of fierce demonstrations and protests—only adds a further ironic twist to his comment. And yet, at the Bicentenary conference, Sterne was discussed almost solely as "one of us," a great philosophical novelist whose work anticipated much in twentieth-century literature and metaphysics—but not, as I recall, the thoughts of Vietnam protesters or counterculture students.

The lesson here is not that Traugott and the conference were wrong, but that they were trapped, as are all readers, by the cultural, economic, political, and moral baggage we carry so lightly as often to be unaware of its burdens. To be sure, one might suggest that Traugott, in this instance, seems more free than I from a hobby-horsical concern, namely, a desire to condemn poor Uncle Toby in the light of a post-Vietnam morality. Several decades of postmodernist theory have taught us, perhaps, to be more perceptive. Behind Traugott's certainty about his reading of Toby we can trace an assurance that "good" nations fight "just" wars (Traugott was 18 years old when World War II started); and behind his repetition of "irrelevant," lurks a political confrontation with his students, the word *relevant* having been the shibboleth for the student movement of the 1960s. In short, neither side in the dispute can lay claim to objectivity.

When in the following year my own study of Toby appeared in *Laurence Sterne as Satirist*, Traugott's only published comment was that interpretations of *Tristram* had become so strained he had even heard of a reading that actually condemned Toby! His was not an isolated protest; the chorus of defenders of Toby showed remarkable uniformity in arguing that I had smeared one of the most lovable creations in all of English literature.

Chastened, if not yet fully convinced, let me approach Uncle Toby somewhat differently almost a quarter century later. Sterne's dismissal of rationalism, as represented by Walter, seems naturally to lead us to what appears at first sight a valid eighteenth-century alternative to it: the endorsement of feeling or sensibility. The dichotomies are well-established: the intuitive and instinctual versus the calculating; the heart versus the head; the social versus the selfish; benevolence versus self-interest. If Walter's fate, the fate of rationalism, is endless discourse about a white bear, surely Toby's inability (or disinclination) to participate in his constructs would be a step in the right direction. The heart—by which one usually means sympathy, pity, empathy, fellow-feeling, benevolence—steers us in the right direction, and we need only follow it rather than flawed reason to arrive at the good—the moral—life.

What, then, could possibly induce Nietzsche to condemn this "morality of pity"? One reason is that he sees the "heart" as the seat of self-indulgent solipsism, the celebration of one's instinctive self, perceived as gentle and gentile, rather than bestial; for him, morality consisted primarily in the discipline of self: "All those who do not have themselves sufficiently under their own control and do not know morality as a continual self-command and self-overcoming . . . involuntarily become glorifiers of the good, pitying, benevolent impulses, of that instinctive morality which has no head but seems to consist solely of heart and helping hands. It is, indeed, in their interest to cast suspicion on a morality of rationality and to make of that other morality the only one" (*Human*, 322). What Nietzsche encapsulates here is the history of moral philosophy from the early eighteenth-century writings of Lord Shaftesbury, through the great romantic flowering, to the nineteenth-century's end in his own lonely rage against his age and its morality of pity. It is our moral world as well, a secular, human-centered age of sympathy and benevolence, fellow-feeling, and charity toward all, the result of listening to our hearts rather than our heads. Or just possibly, these words do not quite describe our age.

Lord Shaftesbury, in his *Characteristics of Men, Manners, Opinions, Times* (1711) essentially argues that the human being possesses an innate moral tendency that embraces the good and eschews the bad. It is an argument against the received moral philosophy associated with Christianity: since the Fall in Eden, the human being has a flawed moral tendency, one that will embrace the bad and eschew the good, unless redirected by faith and Grace, reason and revelation, church and state. All are required to reverse the fall in Eden, and it is this necessary *external* aid that Shaftesbury calls into question. Placed within this polemical context, Shaftesbury's "sentimentalism" is not a revolt against rationalism, but against Christianity, which has a deep-seated, doctrinal distrust of the unaided human mind, although in the eighteenth century it did define a role for "right reason" (reason "informed" by Grace) in the human scheme. The crucifixion of Christ is directly related to the need for intercession (aid) after the Fall, and *Christ* continued to play, as might be expected, a role in eighteenth-century concepts of *Christ*ianity—although not in the systems of non-believers, Unitarians, and Shaftesburians.

Nietzsche's condemnation of the morality of pity is closely linked, I believe, to the misrepresentation of Christian ideology among both rationalists and sentimentalists of the eighteenth century, who are, in reality, indistinguishable to him. In his brilliant attack on the comfortable Christianity of David Strauss, for example, Nietzsche strikes a note very similar to Swift's attack on nominal Christianity. Nietzsche's emphasis is always on Strauss's distortions of the fundamental *irrationalism* of Christianity, his shift in belief from the Son of God as the blood-soaked sacrificial lamb of atonement, who restores a relationship between the human and divine, to the soft pieties of a Jesus who is the "human" model of humility, gentleness, kindness, *and nothing more*.[4] I am not arguing that Nietzsche believed in this "primitive" Christ, but merely that intellectually he preferred that figure to the "modern" one. And behind this preference is Nietzsche's suspicion concerning human moral sufficiency, that wonderful irony of observation he turned on all claims of human moral righteousness.

Rationalism is the assertion of human sufficiency; sentimentalism is that sufficiency acting in the moral sphere: together, they bear the brunt of Nietzsche's philosophical scorn.

As sometimes happens in discourse, metaphor can lead us astray; one example of this is the seemingly physiological distinction between head and heart. It is worth reminding ourselves, therefore, that the heart is only a blood-pump; while it may react to certain stimuli by altering its pumping rate, words such as *heartfelt, heartache,* and *heartbreak* are all metaphors for mental responses. Feelings, in brief, are ideas (and ideas are feelings), no less so for possibly being more difficult to articulate or justify. The premise behind Shaftesbury's writings, the sentimental movement that ensued, and, ultimately, our own modern morality, is that the individual as a thinking being, freed from ancient myths of depravity, is capable of leading a moral life without external assistance; that the human mind, especially when disguised as "the humane heart," is a *sufficient* instrument.[5]

If, then, faith in the individual is a mode of rationalist thinking, one might suggest with some validity that nineteenth-century romanticism is a development of eighteenth-century rationalism, and not, as usually suggested, a reaction against it. Insofar as romanticism invests heavily in the human capacity to thrive as moral creatures independent of institutional (religious or communal) assistance, and insofar as it places enormous faith in individual human response to ethical dilemmas, its opponent is not the rationalist, but the orthodox Christian. With this in mind, we can reexamine Sterne's relationship with the romantic period that followed his own; Nietzsche again offers a useful clue.

The nineteenth-century romantic writer most often associated with Sterne is the German humorist, Jean Paul (Richter), whose theories of humor and irony entered the English tradition by way of Coleridge. His ideas underlie, for example, Coleridge's well-known evaluation of *Tristram Shandy*: "Hence in humor the little is made great, and the great little, in order to destroy both, because all is equal in contrast with the infinite. . . . Hence the tender feeling connected with the *humors* or hobby-horses of a man. . . . Acknowledgment of the hollowness and farce of the world, and its disproportion to the godlike within us" (Howes, 354). What is defined in these famous—if somewhat incoherent—sentences is romantic irony, an irony that dismisses all differences between earthly things, since everything is rendered equally insignificant in comparison to the divine. A concomitant to romantic irony is an attitude of universal tolerance toward the world and its diversity, which we perceive with God's vision rather than our human eyes.

Romantic irony may profitably be compared to a competing mode of ironic discourse, one particularly associated with eighteenth-century satire, an irony that depends on the *intolerance* inherent in distinction and discrimination—that is, in measurement. Because the undisputed master satirists of the English tradition, Dryden, Swift, and Pope, self-consciously echo Roman antecedents, Lucian, Petronius, Horace, Juvenal, and Persius in particular, as the first great practitioners of this mode of irony, we may perhaps label it Augustan irony, without being accused of a careless taxonomy. One crucial difference between Augustan and romantic ironists is that the former are very dubious about the moral or aesthetic efficacy of Coleridge's "godlike within us." To the contrary, they argue that human pretensions to "godlike" vision (or visions) account for much of the "farce and hollowness" of a world that refuses to acknowledge the infinite distance between the human and the divine. Anglican Christianity posits the doctrine of a "divine residue," the human capacity, through Christ, to respond to God's grace through faith. It does not suggest, however, that fallen human beings ("In *Adam*'s fall, / We sinned *All*," as schoolchildren learned with the letter "A") could separate themselves from their own interests, biases, bodies, ideas, hopes, and passions, long enough to become "godlike," could rise above humanity to become angels, or—in Swift's wonderful image in *Gulliver's Travels*—rational horses. Human beings who think they are sufficiently rational act like another part of a horse's anatomy; Augustan irony gives trenchant substance to this observation.

My comparison between romantic and Augustan irony gives a particular edge to Nietzsche's curt dismissal of Jean Paul: "Jean Paul knew a great deal but had no science, was skilled in all kinds of artistic artifices but had no art, found almost nothing unenjoyable but had no taste, possessed feeling and seriousness but . . . poured over them a repulsive broth of tears, he had indeed wit—but unhappily far too little to satisfy his ravenous hunger for it" (*Human*, 334–35). One might surmise that Nietzsche's comments are strictly aesthetic, but I suspect a more philosophical reason accounts for his high praise of Sterne, followed soon after by this assault on Jean Paul, one that centers on the distinction between Augustan and romantic irony just outlined—and, with my earlier discussion of Yorick in mind, one best revealed in the phrase: "[he] had no taste." The universal tolerance that accepts all behavior as equal, that does not measure, and does not weigh, is an attitude Nietzsche everywhere deplores, because it entails either a rationalistic or sentimental faith in the individual mind. Nietzsche's insight, born of his own predilection for the Augustan mode of irony (as it survived in Goethe) might tempt us to question the dominant critical consensus that links Sterne to Jean Paul and thus to preromanticism or romanticism.

Uncle Toby is Sterne's version of Shaftesbury's ideal moral being; not only is his morality instinctual and innate, but his religion is as well, for Toby possesses an uninstructed providential faith (see, for example, his solution to the cause of long noses [III.41.240/284]), even while he embodies Shaftesbury's tendency toward moral secularism. For Sterne, steeped in Restoration polemics against Puritan dissenters (which he turned on the Methodists in his own sermons), the connection seemed natural; those who found God's presence outside of orthodox (that is, sanctioned) occurrences were suspect, not only as self-deceivers, but, equally, as a threat to the true religion. Such combinations of opposing tendencies, piety and iconoclasm, the "god within" and self-deception, best define Sterne's creation. On the one hand, Toby would not "hurt a fly"; on the other, he takes extra time and care dressing for his reenactment of the siege of Lille, in which some 23,000 soldiers are killed or wounded (VI.24.450–51/543–44). Similarly, Toby's warm heart embraces all humankind, yet when the widow Wadman seeks the satisfactions of a frank sexual embrace, he is unable or unwilling to respond. Sterne's embodiment of the new doctrines of sensibility within the very old satiric figure of the *miles gloriosus* (the strutting soldier) would seem to be a carefully chosen strategy, a restaging of the satiric gambit by which claims to special virtues (courage, foreknowledge, communication with God, strict piety, or sexual purity) are *measured* against the "weakness of the vessel" that makes them.

Bearing in mind that our "instruction" as twentieth-century readers is always toward tolerance rather than measurement, acceptance rather than discrimination (the connotations of which are today almost entirely negative, despite the cognate, "discriminating," for a person of "taste"), it is difficult to bring the issue to a "fair trial." Like Don Quixote, who was almost certainly more a madman in Cervantes's eyes than in our own, Uncle Toby has taken on a life independent of his author and the book in which he appears. For much of the nineteenth century, the image of Toby is of a plump, kindly gentleman seated next to the widow, gazing with fondness (but not appetite) into her romantic (but hardly lascivious) eye—the painting of this scene by C. R. Leslie in the early years of the century was often reproduced, not only as an engraving, but also in porcelain and as a ceramic pot-lid. Another favorite subject for these pot-lids was Dickens's Mr. Pickwick, and it was with this strand of harmless and humorous English eccentrics (and the "lovable" Quixote behind them all) that Toby became almost inextricably entwined.

Perhaps the nineteenth century was comfortable with the fact that Toby's amours remain "innocent." Indeed, Leslie's image of Toby is a perfect icon for sentimentalists of any era, a frozen moment of eternal courtship, never to progress further than the sitting position. But, as Corporal Trim so artfully reminds us, the sexual body is rarely content with *upright*-ness: "I was shewing Mrs. *Bridget* our fortifications, and in going too near the edge of the fossè, I unfortunately slip'd in. . . . [A]nd being link'd fast . . . arm in arm with Mrs. *Bridget*, I dragg'd her after me, by means of which she fell backwards soss against the bridge" (III.24.210/248). Or again, Trim's courtship of the fair beguine:

> As she continued rub-rub-rubbing—I felt it spread from under her hand, an' please your honour, to every part of my frame——
> The more she rubb'd, and the longer strokes she took——the

more the fire kindled in my veins——till at length, by two or
three strokes longer than the rest——my passion rose to the highest pitch——I seiz'd her hand——
——And then, thou clapped'st it to thy lips, Trim, said my
uncle Toby——and madest a speech.
Whether the corporal's amour terminated precisely in the way
my uncle Toby described it, is not material. . . . (VIII.22.574–75/
703–4)

These scenes are not to be found in the many editions of the
Beauties of Sterne (selected "for the heart of sensibility") that enabled
nineteenth-century readers to recreate *Tristram* in their own image;
nor will one find similar scenes or innuendoes in Dickens or any other
nineteenth-century English fiction-writers—except those "privately
printed" for "gentlemen's clubs." In fact, one rarely finds such an exuberant and *happy* enjoyment of sexuality until very recently in western
European literature, although it was present, often enough, in literature prior to the eighteenth century. Moreover, it is important to note
that one of the two episodes comes very late in the work, long after
Sterne had been severely chastised for his bawdiness by reviewers who,
mindful of both his clerical robes and the changing tastes of midcentury Britain, told him to mine his sentimental vein instead.

We might, of course, subject Sterne to posthumous psychoanaly-
sis in an attempt to explain the persistence of bawdiness in *Tristram
Shandy*, but it might also be of some value simply to observe that
among the numerous polarities of the work, the one between sexual
innocence and sexual knowledge is certainly the most pervasive. Toby
and the appropriately designated *Corporal* Trim play out this opposition at almost every turn. Much of Trim's behavior is in obvious contrast to Toby's ignorance about women; and Trim's dramatic
revelation of the motives of the widow as *Tristram Shandy* draws
toward its conclusion suggests that Sterne consciously emphasizes the
contest between them:

——God bless your honour! cried the Corporal——what has a
woman's compassion to do with a wound upon the cap of a man's
knee. . . .

"The knee is such a distance from the main body—whereas the groin, your honour knows, is upon the very *curtin* of the *place*." (IX.31.643/802–3)

Actually, two conflicts are found in these sentences, the first between compassion (the "morality of pity") and sexual appetite, the second between sexuality and Toby's military establishment. In both instances it seems insufficient to suggest that the oppositions encompass human diversity without measurement. Rather, they clash dramatically with one another (and the reenactment of battles is the well-chosen emblem for this clash), creating a world not merely of position and counterposition, but of victors and victims. Toby's virtue—his sentimentalism and feeling heart—fails in its encounter with human desire; indeed, his most overt sexual response comes when he sits by himself in the corner of the sentry box, puffing on Trim's cannon/water-pipes (VI.28). The essence of the "morality of pity," Sterne observed, is, paradoxically, self-indulgence rather than a legitimate response to the "other," which is possibly one reason why more traditional moral systems (such as Christianity) do not trust the unaided human heart (that is, the human mind). Even more to the point, Toby's militarism recalls the reality of human polarities: rather than tolerance of the claims and oppositions of others, enforced capitulation has been the order of human history. When we consider the individual effort expended every day to convince those around us to share our opinions and perceptions—and the heat generated even by our "opinion" that toleration is the fuel of morality—we begin to sense exactly why Toby's militarism (remember that the bowling green originates in his desire better to "explain" himself) is not merely a contrast to his sentimentalism, but a comment on it as well.

Toby's fear of sexuality and his embrace of warfare do not render him a villain, any more than Walter's foolishness is evil or vicious. Satire has certainly attacked vice in its day, but just as frequently has directed its barbs toward human folly and that self-blindness which produces it. Toby is fully capable of honest warmth toward some of his fellow creatures, Walter, Trim, Le Fever, most obviously. It strikes me as purposely ironic, however, to describe a person who, while sympathetic toward a fly, reenacts with pleasure battles in which tens of thousands are killed or wounded. Still, we need not quarrel with Toby's treatment of Le Fever—despite the obvious comic wink of his name.[6] But Toby's inability to respond to the widow Wadman, his love of mankind that is baffled by the appetite of one woman, remains highly suspect in a work already rife with male impotence and inadequacy.

The courtship is concluded at the very end of *Tristram Shandy*, where Walter seems to deliver his own version of "Lillabullero" to Toby's failure. Interestingly, Walter's words come to Sterne—without acknowledgment—from Pierre Charron's *Of Wisdom* (1612), a work that summarizes the views of Sterne's beloved Montaigne; quite possibly, he had Charron also in hand for the discussion of procreation with which he had begun *Tristram Shandy* eight years earlier.[7] The passage is prefaced by a capsule summation of what we have learned about Walter in the course of the work, namely, that he is a man "whose way was to force every event in nature into an hypothesis, by which means never man crucified TRUTH at the rate he did" (IX.32.644/804). What is interesting is the glance at militarism in the word "force"; and, just as significant, the Christian allusion, by which Sterne keeps us aware—as a good satirist will—of the normative values that are never out of his mind, however obliquely they establish their measurements of the topsy-turvy world of Shandy Hall. The crucifixion of Christ, of the Word, of Truth, is Christianity's own fable about the human struggle over ideas; Christ crucified (and Christ triumphant, for that matter) hardly bodes well for the notion that the human mind can either hover above opinions or hold an opinion comfortably without wanting to impose it, by force if necessary, on another.

Walter cuts to the heart of the problem, the human dependence on copulation, on the interaction between *self* and *other*, for the continuance of the species: "——THAT provision should be made for continuing the race of so great, so exalted and godlike a Being as man—I am far from denying—but philosophy speaks freely of every thing; and therefore I still think and do maintain it to be a pity, that it should be done by means of a passion which bends down the faculties, and turns all the wisdom, contemplations, and operations of the soul backwards. . . ." Walter then directs his comments at Mrs. Shandy, blasting a passion that "couples and equals wise men with fools, and makes us come out of our caverns and hiding-places more like satyrs and four-footed beasts than men." Why, he asks, "did the delicacy of *Diogenes* and *Plato* so recalcitrate" against sex if it's a natural instinct, and "wherefore, when we go about to make and plant a man, do we put out the candle?" Moreover, and particularly pertinent for the reader of Sterne's bawdy text, why are all "the parts thereof—the congredients—the preparations—the instruments . . . held as to be conveyed to a cleanly mind by no language, translation, or periphrasis whatever?" This is one of Walter's most sustained orations, and it reaches a magnificent level of diatribe in its closing sentence, directed at Toby: "—— The act of killing and destroying a man, continued my father raising his voice . . . is glorious—and the weapons by which we do it are honourable——We march with them upon our shoulders——We strut with them by our sides——We gild them——We carve them——We inlay them——We enrich them——Nay, if it be but a *scoundril* cannon, we cast an ornament upon the breech of it—" (IX.33.644–45/ 806–7).

I quote at length because almost all the themes of *Tristram Shandy*, certainly all those involving Uncle Toby, coalesce in Walter's final oration. Both for Charron and Sterne, the target appears to be both conscious and unconscious denigrations of human sexuality, brilliantly embodied in the final chiasmic polarity that holds ludicrous and shameful the procreative act begetting life, and glorious, the murderous act ending it. In Shandean terms, the dichotomy we have thus far explored, "heads" versus "hearts," turns out to be woefully inadequate, failing to account for the human "loins," or, in Charron's fine phrase, for the "fever and furious passion [which], as it is naturall, so is it . . . common to all . . . this copulation of the male and female."[8]

Walter lays the blame on philosophy and language for their joint failure to discover a proper attitude toward human sexuality. His addition to Charron's argument, the invocation of Diogenes and Plato, gives the Florida annotators some difficulty,[9] but we might simply take both as representative of the inadequacies of classical philosophy. Christianity's complaint against Plato and the other pre-Christian philosophers is repeated again and again in the sermons and discourses of the age, Sterne's among them, and most often appears couched in the rhetoric of pragmatism: classical philosophers fail to grasp the *real* human condition, because their various warring dualisms (life and death, cause and effect, reason and passion) have been enormously complicated—and potentially restored to unity—by the sacrificial intervention of Christ, about whom classical philosophers obviously knew nothing. This same complaint is inherent in Sterne's juxtaposition of Walter's funeral oration with Trim's, the one randomly compounded of useless classical fragments, the other replete with biblical echoes that speak directly to the heart (that is, to the mind) and its desire for immortality; and it recurs in the contrast between practical and polemic divinity, although here it is "Christian" versus "Christian," right belief versus practical application. Trim, the successful lover, the practical expositor of the fifth commandment, *satisfies* in his brief funeral comments our "fever and furious passion"—as Susannah well understands.

Throughout *Tristram Shandy*, Sterne challenges the false modesties of language, the enormous moral stock human beings invest in circumventing the sounding of certain "four-letter" words—or even the imagining of their sound, not to speak of their import. In doing so, he has placed his finger directly upon the *place* (or "in the pye" [see, VIII.11.550/670]), highlighting our continuing inability to convey these natural appetites "to a cleanly mind." Our most common circumlocution, for example, *sexual intercourse*, serves about as well as a cold shower to embody the "fever and furious passion"; *fuck*, on the other hand, if not dulled by repetition, conveys it well, as the nuns of Andoüillets discover, when they capture both the spirit and the letters of the word, despite breaking it into *fou* and *ter* (VII.24–25). Sterne's point is validated by the "twinge" I am certain every reader just felt, even in this liberated age, on seeing *one* word in my last sentence— assuming that the publisher allows the sentence to stand. Sexual hypocrisy (and the verbal hypocrisy that accompanies it) is not simply false piety or priggishness. Far more significant, it is the failure to acknowledge—to give language to—the essence of self as a relation to others, a failure Sterne finds as enervating to one's personal life, as destructive to society, and, ultimately, as serious a threat to heavenly expectations, as would be an equally blind attitude toward spiritual or intellectual hypocrisy. Throughout *Tristram Shandy*, Sterne confronts us with a language that forces the sexual nature of ourselves and others into our consciousness. At times, readers are forced into an awareness the characters do not share; just as often, they may reach an awareness they will admit only with reluctance and embarrassment, uncertain whether other readers are "seeing" the same thing. Sterne knows all this and wants us to realize with him that much more is at stake in our language of sexual reference and circumlocution than a bawdy joke.

Sexuality has the capacity to infuse the most innocent words—*nose, stick, crevice, thing, place, trench*—with connotations that link them to the "fever and furious passion." While any hobby-horse can create this same "leakage" in denotation, (for example, Toby's misunderstanding of "bridge" or "place"), what Sterne illustrates is that sex is *everyone's* hobby-horse—Madam's and Sir's, as well as his Reverence's (that is, the Clergy). Sterne designs for his readers a game of sexual discovering, recovering, and uncovering, played out between the poles of ardent curiosity about the *other* and self-absorption with the *self*. The failure to find an adequate response results in the loss of Strasbourg, and of community more generally, with its implied promise of family and loved ones and immortality. Tristram plays the game himself in volume VII, a dance of death through France in which sexual curiosity leads the procession—until Tristram's recall of a sexual failure with Jenny (VII.29) sends him to the other pole, a self-absorption that will turn him away from Nannette's "cursed slit" in her petticoat, back to the writing of Toby's amours—his "last hope" for immortality.

Tristram's excursion into France, to which I return in chapter 8, runs parallel to Toby's story; both end with an evasion of love, in contrast to Trim's story of the fair beguine (situated between Tristram's flight and Toby's amours), in which love is offered and accepted. Sterne seems to me to question this evasion, both here and in *A Sentimental Journey*, even though the *only* virtue associated with our "fever and furious passion" since the emergence of sentimentalism seems to be our capacity to deny the body through repression, to distance ourselves from the offending member(s) of the opposite gender. Rest assured, I do not believe Sterne is advocating sexual anarchy or orgiastic indulgence. What he does seem to argue, however, is that a society more ashamed of its sexuality than of its violence, a society always ready to make war but ashamed of making love, is in moral and social peril.

Twentieth-century America seems to have succumbed to this peril, evidenced not only in our celebration of violence in general, but, even more worrisome, in the persistent manner in which violence accompanies our sexuality. Moreover, our "open" discussion of sexuality in the media disguises the reality of our enormous repression as a society; the ratings that drive these discussions are surely proportionate to the titillation (adolescent and sterile as it might be, as in the case of the nuns of Andoüillets) that comes from discussing repressed subjects. Sterne's search, to the contrary, seems to be for a union of male and female that is open, honest, and physically adult: a celebration of the "fever and furious passion" as a divine gift, equal to the gifts of "head" and "heart." It is, by and large, a futile—albeit primarily humorous—search. And its emblem, we might say, is Trim's wonderful flourish of his stick in chapter 4 of the final volume. For Toby it is a thousand syllogisms in defense of celibacy; for the good Shandean reader, who has a doubt as to whether "stick" means "stick" and nothing more or less, the Corporal's celebration of "liberty" seems as badly misread (miswritten) by Toby, as is his conclusion to the story of the fair beguine.[10]

Toby's role as Shaftesbury's moral "man of feeling" establishes a dichotomy between sentiments of love and the physical manifestations of it that he is unable to bridge. In *A Sentimental Journey*, Sterne puts the dichotomy into French: "L'amour n'est *rien* sans sentiment. Et le sentiment est encore *moins* sans amour." ("Love is nothing without sentiment. And sentiment is still less without love.")[11] One is reminded of the chiasmic structure in the "Abuses of Conscience" sermon, a legitimate paraphrase of which might be: "Religion is nothing without morality. And morality is still less without religion." For Sterne, sentimentality is a morality without religion, a moral impasse in which

Uncle Toby and the widow Wadman, Tristram and Nannette, are forever separated because the "fever and furious passion" is never adequately acknowledged by those who locate morality (the control of choices and actions) solely within themselves. Nannette's "slit" will be completely sewn up in the nineteenth century, and the widow will be taught to repress her appetites until even the hint that she wants to glimpse what Toby has under his breeches will make her a "fallen woman." This is certainly serious damage inflicted on one half of the human equation, and Sterne is perceptive in associating the decline of institutional religion, and the subsequent rise of moral self-sufficiency, with the nineteenth-century's psychological epidemic of female repression. Sterne's second insight is that the damage caused by the doctrine of moral self-sufficiency befalls men and women equally, although at first glance it might seem otherwise.

The only character who is dramatically not *self-sufficient* is Corporal Trim, Toby's "body" servant, and, in almost every way, a seemingly dependent character. For example, he reads Yorick's sermon, not his own; he shadows Toby in reenacting the battles on the bowling green; he makes love to Bridget because Toby is courting her mistress; he seconds his efforts concerning Le Fever. But Trim is at the same time a *master* and not a *servant* of sexual language, fully aware— as are, naturally enough, all the women of *Tristram Shandy*—of the difference between the right end of a woman and the wrong (II.6). Language fails Toby from the very beginning in this regard; in confusing the "wrong" and "right" ends, let us remind ourselves, Toby is not failing to distinguish between head and heart, or even head (heart) from groin. Rather, given two cavities in the vicinity, he does not seem fully cognizant of the distinct uses of each.

The failure to make certain discriminations can, as in this instance, discontinue the species, and echoes of anal intercourse (and, perhaps, of a certain tendency to homoeroticism and violent penetration) reverberate not only in this passage, but throughout *Tristram Shandy*. These echoes add to the idea of sterility hovering over the Shandy heads, as well as to the image of violence behind the bowling green, insofar as sexual penetration of the natural receptacle becomes instead the forced entry of a physical assault.[12] Keep in mind, the nature of warfare, siege warfare in particular. The aim of the besiegers is to approach the *center of the place*, secretly if possible, perhaps by using trenches and underground tunnels, until they gather with enough power to penetrate the fortress. Remember also, that when Toby goes into the country to begin building his fortified towns, Sterne portrays the event in erotic terms: "Never did lover post down to a belov'd mistress with more heat and expectation, than my uncle *Toby* did, to enjoy this self-same thing in private" (II.5.98/113). In addition, a good Shandean reader by this time will hardly grant innocence to the "rough holly" and "thickset flowering shrubs" surrounding the bowling green. And let us also recall that *Toby* was a slang term for buttocks in the eighteenth century, and *siege* a slang term for anus. Amidst these confusing (bisexual?) signals, Sterne seems clearly to anticipate Freud's concept of displacement, but comes to it from a moral rather than psychological direction.

Moral self-sufficiency, the Shaftesburian morality, was more and more talked about as the century progressed, and even within the Anglican church compromises in the name of moderation and accommodation gave the idea some credence, despite its inherent conflict with institutional religion. Sterne came to associate self-sufficiency with warfare, perhaps because he simply recast all opponents of his viewpoint as "arguers and quarrellers" against the peace of a centrist position. This is certainly a common enough rhetorical ploy in Swift, from whom Sterne seems to have learned much about polemics, including, of course, the posture that he was not, like his opponents, a polemical divine. But it is also possible that Sterne found in the passage Walter quotes from Charron so stark an embodiment of the errors of moral self-sufficiency (the primary subject of the "Abuses of Conscience" sermon, we recall), that his creation of Toby from the beginning was directed toward a climactic use of Charron against him at the end of the work.

Indeed, toward the end of volume VI, when Sterne first turns his full attention to Toby, he anticipates Charron's final comment in "*My Uncle* TOBY's *apologetical* oration" (chap. 32), written in "*justification of his own principles and conduct in wishing to continue the war.*" As with the passage from Charron, the "Apology" is an unacknowledged borrowing, in this instance, from two sources, *Don Quixote* and Robert Burton's *Anatomy of Melancholy* (1621). Perhaps no two books were closer to Sterne's heart or head, and hence his intertwined use of both at this juncture may convey special meaning. At the beginning of this chapter, I spent some time discussing two modes of irony, Augustan and romantic. If we reduce "irony" to one of its fundamental requirements, "distance," all borrowings in a text set up ironic possibilities: we have a *distance* between the original context and the present context, and a second *distance* between the author who knows he is borrowing and readers (or characters) who might not. To be sure, the entire "Apology" seems a marvel of romantic irony, in that it weighs two polar extremes and seems in the end unwilling to resolve them: *"soft and gentle"* creatures, *"born to love, to mercy, and kindness,"* are not shaped for war; yet, war is a "necessity" of principle and honour, a field of courage and bravery (VI.32.462/557). This is the paradox Toby defends and thousands of readers have accepted over the years, a paradox that seems to be a certitude of civilized life: the citizen soldier, the goodhearted, reluctant warrior, whose cause is always just, and who fights savagely, although only for hearth and heaven. It is perhaps an unspoken irony of this portrait that foot soldiers who have seen *actual combat* rarely come away with their certitude intact, not even those fortunate enough to fight in wars that history validates.

The dismantling of a romantic reading of Toby's "Apology" need not, however, rely on personal or anecdotal experience. Sterne's borrowings create an irony of the sort I have labeled Augustan, in that a knowledge of them will lead one to reevaluate Toby's text. By withholding this information, Sterne tempts us into what proves to be an untenable position, admiration for Toby. This admiration is based on a lack of requisite knowledge, a reliance on such dubious concepts (all echoing a morality without religion) as "Nature" and "Necessity," and, above all, a predilection to believe that we can read not only the document before us, but the human heart as well. Toby's "apologetical oration" is a case study in the failure of the Shaftesburian school of moral sensibility.

Hearts

From Cervantes, Sterne borrows a portion of Don Quixote's early defense of knight-errantry (not soldiering) over the profession of scholar; his madness at this early point in the book seems readily apparent: "It is then no longer to be doubted, but that this Exercise and Profession surpasses all others that have been invented by Man, and is so much the more honourable, as it is more expos'd to Dangers. . . . [The] Object and End is Peace, which is the greatest Blessing Man can wish for in this Life. . . . This Peace is the true End of War."[13] The paradox that tries to encompass the universe in its oppositions dissolves in ridicule when the speaker and the subject are fully known; Toby's speech concludes in the same comic (or bathetic) explosion of the paradoxical: "heaven is my witness . . . that the pleasure I have taken in these things,—and that infinite delight, in particular, which has attended my sieges in my bowling green, has arose within me, and I hope in the corporal too, from the consciousness we both had, that in carrying them on, we were answering the great ends of our creation" (VI.32.462/557). Surely this pompous conclusion asks, indeed demands of us, that we measure the activities on the bowling green against *whatever* might be considered the "great ends" of a human life. As with all satiric victims, Uncle Toby comes up very short, culpably short, when measured against the yardstick a good satirist is always able to provide.

Toby's survey of the difficulties of a soldier's life are lifted from Burton's famous diatribe against war in "Democritus to the Reader," his heavily satirical introduction to the *Anatomy*. Toby talks of honor, Burton of soldiers who "prostitute their lives and limbs." And Yorick's comment is a much mollified version of Burton's: "what plague, what fury brought so devilish, so brutish a thing as war first into men's minds? Who made so soft & peaceable a creature, born to love, mercy, meekness, so to rave, rage like beasts, & run on to their own destruction?" Moreover, while Toby significantly reserves his anger over the Trojan War for that "bitch" Helen, Burton lets us know that even in the seventeenth century there were people ready to consider the real cost of war; according to his accounting, "The siege of *Troy* lasted ten years eight months, there died 870,000 Grecians, 670,000 Trojans, at the taking of the City, and after were slain 276,000 men, women, and children, of all sorts." Burton, too, leaves us with a sentence that serves well to measure Toby's own inane conclusion: "Which is yet more to be lamented, they persuade them this hellish course of life is holy."[14] Rest assured, I have only scratched the surface of Burton's fierce diatribe against wars, which begin he suggests, *"by the persuasion of a few debauched, hair-brain, poor, dissolute, hungry captains* [Toby's rank], *parasitical fawners, unquiet Hotspurs, restless innovators, green heads, to satisfy one man's private spleen, lust, ambition, avarice, &c."*

Although we have been told that Toby is "not eloquent," Tristram here informs us that this oration is evidence to "the contrary" (VI.31.458/553). Certainly, the oration is filled with rhetorical gestures—most particularly, the rhetorical question. In fact, after the two-paragraph exordium, the next three paragraphs consist almost entirely of questions addressed to Walter, and the peroration is also in the form of questions, these directed to Yorick. We might exercise our wit for a moment by provoking Toby and Tobyphiles with answers they do not expect. For example, perhaps it does "bespeak [him] cruel" that his heart "panted for war," despite his *belief* that it aches also for war's distresses; perhaps had he panted a shade more for the distresses than for the engagement, he would not have been so ready to fight. Or again, his definition of war is amazingly naïve (and obtuse): "For what is war? what is it, *Yorick*, when fought as ours has been, upon principles of *liberty*, and upon principles of *honour*——what is it, but the getting together of quiet and harmless people, with their swords in their hands, to keep the ambitious and the turbulent within bounds?" (VI.32.462/557). Setting aside the obvious, that both sides in a war claim "liberty" and "honour" to be on their side, Toby's vague division here between the quiet and the ambitious is given startling cogency later in the work, when Toby defines war, "and particularly that branch of it which we have practised together in our bowling-green," as having no object "but to shorten the strides of AMBITION, and intrench the lives and fortunes of the *few*, from the plunderings of the *many*" (IX.8.610/753). It is Sterne, not I, who italicizes the two words that remove war from the "humanity and fellow-feeling" Toby invokes in his oration, two words that place war where it truly belongs, among privilege and inequity and the preservation of property and wealth. Many years ago, I pointed out that whatever "humanity" means to Toby, it does not encompass the masses, since his fellow-feeling is limited to *few* rather than to *many* "fellows." In all the many readings of Uncle Toby as a sentimental hero, no one mentions this passage, much less attempts to explain it. Yet Sterne seems to have pointed his moral by underscoring his manuscript; and he offers the sentence in a chapter that, in its final prayer, finally allows the voice of Sterne to overwhelm the voice of Tristram. Toby Shandy is just not as innocent as we have been led to believe.

Far more important than these counterpositions, however, is Sterne's self-conscious use of the rhetorical question to organize the "Apology." The single most important question behind Sterne's exploration of sentimentalism by means of Uncle Toby is whether we can know ourselves sufficiently to lead unaided moral lives. Toby's desire to reconcile or justify the contradictions he reads in himself leads to a series of questions he wants answered on the basis of brotherly affection and Christian charity. Walter and Yorick are asked to accept his reconstruction of childhood, to accept his contradictions, and to accept his dubious invocations of "NATURE" and "NECESSITY" (again, Sterne uses his typography to emphasize his point). Like Tristram in volume I (chap. 23), Toby would like a Momus's glass in his breast, so that his auditors can look inside and read his heart and conclude, as he has already concluded, that his *heart* and *mind* and *hands* are clean. Christianity, however, teaches a different mode of self-examination, one that begins and ends with the impossibility of truly knowing oneself and thus the daily humbling of oneself in communion with God, for only God can read the human heart: "The heart is deceitful above all things, and desperately wicked: who can know it? I the Lord search the heart, I try the reins [that is, the body], even to give every man according . . . to the fruits of his doings" (Jeremiah 17:9–10).

We need not necessarily endorse this orthodoxy to understand Sterne's point: a morality based on the human capacity to know oneself is always going to fall victim to self-interest and self-partiality, to the blindness that ensues because we do not have a window in our breast (or brain)—we cannot know ourselves. If Walter Shandy's rationalist attempt to subdue the world around him demonstrates a mind obviously inadequate to the task, Toby Shandy's quite similar *rationalist* attempt to subdue the world, this time by an appeal to his own *knowledge* of his heart, his pity, his fellow-feeling, also proves inadequate. The world of war continues, the widow Wadman remains unwed, the Shandy line is halted, and moral wisdom continues to elude the best feelings and sympathies that compounded human beings can muster. What separates Walter and Toby most dramatically is Walter's impatience and nervous irritability, his restless movement from theory to theory, as opposed to Toby's stability, his monolithic hobby-horse, his self-satisfaction in the rightness of his cause, the hallmark, perhaps, of the "militiating" mind—as Sterne calls it. In this respect, and in the appeal Toby has so successfully made to so many readers, we may be justified in believing he is the far more dangerous threat to morality than is Walter. That, at any rate, is what Nietzsche seems to suggest:

> With whom does the greatest danger for the whole human future lie? Is it not with the good and just?—with those who say and feel in their hearts: "We already know what is good and just, we possess it too; woe to those who are still searching for it!" (*Zarathustra*, 229)

8

Joy

Character	*Mrs. Shandy*
Foil	*Jenny*
Incident	*The Bed of Justice*
Document	*The Marriage Settlement*
Activity	*Procreating*
Image	*Hogarth's illustration of the Christening*
-Ism	*Pragmatism*

Objections, non-sequiturs, cheerful distrust, joyous mockery—all are signs of health. Everything absolute belongs in the realm of pathology.[1]

The role of women in *Tristram Shandy* has awaited the rise of feminist criticism in order to be recognized. The first important essay in this regard, using perspectives gained from a decade of feminist writing, is Leigh Ehlers's "Mrs. Shandy's 'Lint and Basilicon': The Importance of Women in *Tristram Shandy*."[2] Starting from the simple observation that while Walter is inanely reading Spencer's chapters on circumcision, Mrs. Shandy is beginning the healing process for Tristram's wound by applying lint and basilicon (V.27), Ehlers concludes that the Shandy males, by isolating themselves from women, deny themselves restorative powers that come not from women alone, but from the union of male and female in this world.

A second important essay on the subject is Helen Ostovich's "Reader as Hobby-Horse in *Tristram Shandy*."[3] The opposition between wit and judgment, she argues, is played out between the writer as male, the reader as female; what is required for proper understanding is cooperation between the two.[4] Ehlers and Ostovich unite in stressing the countermanding influence of the women of *Tristram Shandy* on male misdirection; in terms of this discussion, they suggest that Sterne's women, like Yorick, serve a normative role within the upside-down world of his satiric fiction.

This is not to argue that Sterne is a feminist, if by that term we mean an advocate of equality or even, more simply, a person fully conscious of gender-spawned inequities. No male in the eighteenth century could sufficiently escape his age to pass a present litmus test along those lines. But to label Sterne a sexist, as at least one feminist reader has done,[5] seems quite wrong. Sterne does tell jokes at the expense of women, but in a work filled with jokes at the expense of men, excluding women from his satire would be more discriminatory (and patronizing) than not doing so. Sterne does not condescend to the human condition, male or female, and his wit seems amply and equally spread between *Sir* and *Madam*. More to the point, the argument that Sterne scorns Mrs. Shandy's lack of language or intellect is to attribute to him Walter's attitude—a very poor reading, indeed, of the irony of the text.

A more serious complaint against Sterne as a sexist might be couched in these terms: behind his vision of Mrs. Shandy, the widow Wadman, Jenny, Aunt Dinah, female servants, and female readers, is a male fantasy of female promiscuity—the lascivious fallen "daughters of Eve." All Sterne's women (including Mrs. Shandy) have highly developed sexual curiosities and sexual appetites; most if not all seem to be seducers of men, temptresses to dalliance, who take men unwillingly but inevitably from the real business and duty of life. This is, to be sure, a very old complaint against women, solidified for Western civilization in readings of Genesis. It is, however, an inadequate reading of

Sterne's women, and in this chapter, building on what I have already postulated about Walter and Toby, I will explain my reasons for saying so.

What *is* the "real business of life?" We might recall, for example, the passage quoted above in chapter 7, where Toby insists that he and Trim carry out the "great ends" of their creation on the bowling green (VI.32.462/557); or we might recall that for Walter, raising his son is a solemn duty carried out in the *Tristrapædia*, which, unfortunately, grows much more slowly than does Tristram, and hence is useless. In both instances, Sterne conveys the strong suggestion that Walter's intellect and Toby's passion for military activity do *not* adequately engage them in whatever we might want to define as "real life." From this perspective, then, any cessation of their current activities might turn (or tempt) them *toward* real life, rather than away from it, despite delusions to the contrary. In Shandean terms, they would be forced to dismount their hobby-horses in order to get on with the jog-trot of mundane existence.

Because the Shandy males all have hobby-horsical natures, an alternative almost naturally offers itself in the females of the Shandy world. This is not, however, merely a convenience of gender. Rather, it is a strategy that emerges from the inherent nature of the hobby-horse, which is characterized most readily by its solipsistic and monolithic self-containment. Beginning perhaps in jest, but ending always in "downright earnest," the hobby-horse absorbs the self with one's self, and reduces the history of the world to one's bowling green, and the multifold claims of human nature and nurture to the size and proportions of one's own unifying system(s). The movement is always reductive (as in a siege, one "reduces" the fortress) and single-minded, and belligerence permeates the worlds of *both* Walter and Toby, although differently imaged. Swift's famous statement on the reductive urge of the human mind is never very far from Sterne's revisiting of the subject: "But when a man's fancy gets *astride* on his reason, when imagination is at cuffs with the senses, and common understanding as well as common sense, is kicked out of doors; the first proselyte he makes is himself, and when that is once compassed the difficulty is not so great in bringing over others, a strong delusion always operating from *without* as vigorously as from *within*" (*Tale of a Tub*, 82). The first effect of the hobby-horse is self-conviction; the second, is the irresistible urge to convince others to share one's saddle. The hobby-horse refuses to allow the differentness of the *other*; the *other* is rarely if ever allowed to ride peaceably down the King's highway, so insistent is our urge to persuade the world that our construction (and constriction) of reality is the Truth.

Walter does battle with the facts until they conform to his theories, and then with his auditors until they agree with him. Because his theories are absurd and his character humorous, we dismiss his argumentativeness as harmless; informing it, however, is the urge of the demagogue, and citizens of the twentieth century have learned that they dismiss even ludicrous demagogues at their peril. This is the painful lesson Swift learned from the religious wars of the seventeenth century, and certainly accounts for much of the intensity of *Tale of a Tub*. In a somewhat similar fashion, we tend to dismiss Uncle Toby because of the minuteness of his replication of warfare on the bowling green, and his kindness in other, non–hobby-horsical, aspects of his life. Walter's argumentative *reductiveness* is, however, a telling reflection of Toby's *reduction* of warfare's dimensions. The brothers conduct "warfare" in order to *reduce* the threats and potentialities of "otherness"; they strive to convert what is different from themselves into *objects* that can be absorbed (by system) or destroyed (by siege), for in the hobby-horsical world, otherness represents "*objections*," that is, resistance to the order of the belligerent.

Less metaphorically, we are unable to hold opinions without seeking to convert others to them, without obliging others to see the truth we see. As one begins to agree or disagree with the above sentence, the truth of it emerges; Sterne shows us that language always serves position and power, that we are hard-pressed to find modes of expression that do not try to convert opinion into dogma, otherness into sameness. We simply cannot imagine having an opinion that is not true—and, more important, universally acknowledged to be so. (Of course, our "universe," like the Shandy world, is often a mere "four *English* miles diameter" [I.7.11/10].)

Joy

Sentimentalism (the feeling heart) is, perhaps, a mode of expression that seems to promise resistance to the proselytizing urge, because of its solipsistic tendency, but in Sterne's exploration, its intimate connection with militarism uncovers the profound hostility toward others buried in stances of self-absorption; and Toby's failure with the widow Wadman suggests to me the dangerous sterility of a moral system that cannot negotiate a truce between the self and the other. In contrast to sentimentalism's failure, Sterne embodies a viable mode of resistance to solipsism in his females, perhaps because in his eighteenth-century world the argument and counterargument of human life, the strong assertion of self, seemed predominantly male prerogatives. Argumentation and warfare are, as already implied, not unrelated; rhetoric and military tactics are both "sciences for overcoming opposition."

There is, of course, a defensive warfare (for the besieged), but, excepting the amours, Toby is always a besieger; similarly, we might posit a rhetoric that eschews the art of persuasion, but Walter's arguments (and our own) are always designed to convince, rather than to compromise, much less to concur. Rhetoric is the art (or science) of persuading others that we are right; there is no comparable art designed to convince others that they are right—or that we are wrong. More to the point, there is no received rhetorical strategy for expressing our doubts, our suspensions of judgments, our sense of the unknown and unknowable. Judaism (especially in its Gnostic mode) might seem to have conceived such a strategy, but after its initial insight that God is ineffable, it quickly developed the "life and opinions" of that God in great and dogmatic detail. Jesus' efforts to rescue Jewish rhetoric from the Pharisees ended with crucifixion and Paul's dogmatics. Classical skepticism also worked to develop such a rhetoric, but it collapsed on the shoals of human psychology and sophistic quibbles. Above all, our inability to know the other comes up squarely against the pragmatic observation that we cannot continue to live without knowing the other; and the biblical sense of *knowing* gives physiological reinforcement to what might otherwise seem a limited theological, philosophical, or psychological observation.[6]

93

The females of the Shandy world embody Sterne's exploration of social, rhetorical, and, ultimately, moral strategies designed to preserve the uniqueness and integrity of the self, one's differentness, amid the welter of the world's opinions; at the same time, these strategies also establish human sexuality as the model for the self's relations with the other, as opposed to the model of argumentation (conflict), which we too often accept as our sole model of human interaction, including, of course, the *"war* of the sexes." The aim, significantly, is not to assert or celebrate the "Self" (which would await romanticism), but to create and preserve the "Other." This particular paradox, the destructiveness of one mode of self-assertiveness, the fertility of another, is Sterne's guiding insight into human relationships and, of equal importance to him, into the creature's relationship with the Creator.

Before I fall into the common modern error of abstracting Sterne's notions into ethereal linguistic or metaphysical realms, I will return to the mundane by recalling to mind the overwhelming evidence of Sterne's lifelong promiscuity, despite his marriage and clerical robes. He seems to have convinced himself early and often of the "truth" he puts into Yorick's mouth in *A Sentimental Journey*: "[I have] been in love with one princess or another almost all my life, and I hope I shall go on so, till I die, being firmly persuaded, that if ever I do a mean action, it must be in some interval betwixt one passion and another" (*Journey*, 128–29). Sterne's life supports the strong suggestion of *Tristram Shandy* that this generalized affection for women was not merely a question of "head" or "heart," that is, not merely platonic or sentimental. The married clergyman was attracted to the bodies of women not his wife; the insistence, the strength, of this urge, in the face of religious and social sanctions against it, is what Sterne seems most intent on exploring, especially in the closing volumes of *Tristram*, and then in *A Sentimental Journey* as well.

Nor was it merely a matter of intellectual curiosity. During much of the time he was writing *Tristram Shandy*, Sterne thought himself very close to death; indeed, after delivering volumes V and VI to the printer in the fall of 1761, he hastened to France in a desperate effort to restore his failing health, and from that time until his death, his life was, as he foretells in his dedication to volumes I and II, "a constant endeavour to fence against the infirmities of ill health." The weakening of his own body, the concomitant waxing of appetite for the female body, form one distinct pattern of these years. Less evident, perhaps, but equally urgent, the presence of death had to suggest to an eighteenth-century Anglican clergyman—one with a particular distaste for hypocrisy—the coming judgment. Behind Sterne's exploration of male-female relationships is a large modicum of self-examination and self-justification, but his conclusions are no less valid for originating in these eschatological concerns.[7]

Hence a second pattern emerges, one in which sexual repression and sexual frankness dance to a tune that will eventually (in *A Sentimental Journey*) receive the name of Joy. And a third pattern emerges as well in *Tristram Shandy*, a pattern whereby sexual communion is posited as a means (perhaps the only means) of overcoming the world of position and counterposition, endless debate and endless warfare, all of which had ceased, in Sterne's eyes, to energize or validate his own existence. Sterne lodges the secret of overcoming within his female characters, because his viewpoint is consistently that of the self as male, the other as female. To overcome—and I purposely use a favorite Nietzschean word—one asserts the self in the act of choosing to surrender oneself to the other. In *Tristram Shandy*, the process seems always gendered (except in the Le Fever episode), and hence always to revolve around sexuality. However, in so far as what Sterne describes is within a nexus of paradoxical ideas concerning the rebirth of a new person through surrender of the old, it is also a Christian process, although Sterne's emphasis on the body (not only for procreation, but for pleasure as well) might suggest otherwise—especially to those Christians whose faith is emphatically Pauline.

The women of *Tristram Shandy* are not Pauline. Within the English context, they are too late to be puritanical and too early to be Victorian; and the moral bridge between the two eras, the sentimental, is a label we assign to the males of Shandy Hall rather than to its females. What unites Sterne's women—the wife, the widow, the mistress, Aunt Dinah, the servants, the fair beguine, Janatone, and Nannette—is sexual appetite; only the nuns, heirs of St. Paul, resist this bond, although their language betrays them. This being so, it is perhaps not surprising that the primary scene of action for the women of *Tristram Shandy* is the bedroom—indeed, the bed. I have already discussed the opening scene, but it is worth repeating here that Elizabeth is not the butt of Sterne's humor; rather her husband, who cannot produce a child by himself, no matter how hard he concentrates, appears to be Sterne's sole target. Mrs. Shandy will spend considerable time in the early volumes of *Tristram Shandy* in childbed, but her opening question in the marital bed gives birth to the book we hold in our hands; had she not imposed herself on Walter's single-minded purpose, the adult Tristram would have had nothing to wish for. As is so often the case in the work, interruption and digression prove the most fertile ground, while concentrated effort in one direction, which Tristram pleads for in his opening sentence, the straight line of gravity and paternal purposefulness, most often proves sterile. Mrs. Shandy's procreative instincts are far more powerful, it appears, than those of Walter's single-minded and sciatical loins.

The marriage bed and the childbed coalesce into the bed of justice, where we can perhaps best see Mrs. Shandy's function in the Shandy world. As both the term and the practice indicate, the Shandy bed of justice weaves threads of sexuality and judgment (measurement) into a fabric that can sustain and nurture new life. Its origin is twofold. On the one hand, Tristram introduces it within a context of human argumentativeness, it being a process by which a question is "weighed, poized, and perpended——argued upon——canvassed through——entered into, and examined on all sides . . ." (VI.16.434/ 522). This is clearly Walter's world, although Tristram draws a distinction between his heat ("a kind of huff, and a defiance of all mankind") and the "GODDESS of COOLNESS," who supposedly has presided over the deliberations; Tristram wisely eschews any demonstration of her existence.

On the other hand, we are given a historical origin as well, the ancient German practice of deliberating every issue twice, "once drunk and once sober." At stake are "vigour" and "discretion" (or "spirit" and "sobriety"), which, in the Shandy world, becomes a sexual dichotomy: Walter "fixed and set apart the first *Sunday* night in the month, and the *Saturday* night which immediately preceded it"

(VI.17.435/ 523–24) for his beds of justice. This sexuality is, in turn, displaced by Tristram, whose own parallel is to write "all nice and ticklish discussions" one half *full*, and the other half, *fasting*. In each instance, the *pros* and *cons* (VI.17.434/522) of debate, the argument and counterargument of language, are reflected by physical acts, but as is so often the case in *Tristram Shandy*, systematic arrangement is deceptive. While drinking and eating may be practiced in moderation and are susceptible to a compromise between extremes, the sexual act allows no such moderation. We are not asked to examine the *frequency* of sexual activity (which has, from the beginning, been established as regularly infrequent), but rather the quality of judgment prior to intercourse and after it. Moreover, it is not clear which night produces "the understrapping virtue of discretion" and which produces vigor— each partner might have a different answer to that question: "*Quod omne animal post coitum est* triste" ("After intercourse every animal is *sad*"), a hoary sentence usually followed by a humorous exception (for example, women or priests). Tristram quotes the adage apropos of yet another physical dichotomy, the radical heat and radical moisture (V.36.397/475). What Tristram fails to account for with his facile analogies concerning the beds of justice is that the sexual act involves two people, while drunkenness and gluttony and writing only one. This is a family error among Shandy males, for Tristram only repeats Walter's error, but it tells us much about our own view of sexuality that we accept his litany of drunkenness, gluttony, and sexuality (lust) as equivalent indulgences of bodily appetites that must be controlled. As with all arguments by dichotomy, the middle ground is inviting, but Tristram's metaphor of mechanism warns us that satire is afoot: "These different and almost irreconcileable effects, flow uniformly from the wise and wonderful mechanism of nature,—of which,—be her's the honour.——All that we can do, is to turn and work the machine to the improvement and better manufactury of the arts and sciences" (VI.17.436/525). The Swiftian tone here suggests the influence of the Scriblerians on Sterne at this point in volume VI; the Florida editors suggest that the ensuing discussion of Tristram's breeches owes much, in fact, to Cornelius Scriblerus's discussion of the classical antecedents of his son's toys.[8] Swift, Pope, and Sterne all reject the notion that human beings can be explained by mechanistic principles, not because they prefer to glorify the human as "spiritual," but because they believe such principles, did they exist, would not be comprehensible to the flawed minds of human beings.

Similarly, while "nature" is often praised in both *Tristram Shandy* and Scriblerian literature ("First follow Nature," is Pope's cardinal rule of writing), here the modifying "mechanism" and the female pronoun set "nature" in opposition to Providence, which is marked— for the Christian—by antimechanism, by a judicious particularity, and by an energetic intervention into whatever laws of nature we are able to discover. Walter Shandy has attempted to bring his sexuality (and his life) under modes of mechanistic (that is, predictable) control, but he is a target, not a model; Mrs. Shandy and the other women of *Tristram Shandy* do not make the same mistake.

Let us not overheat our imaginations, as Tristram might warn. Sterne is not arguing for sexuality without restraint, or even for that Blakean excess which leads to the palace of wisdom—or the promontory of noses. The notion, however, that sexual appetite could be encompassed within the same moral simplicities that apply to drunkenness, that the relationship between a man and a woman was the same as that between a man and a bottle, he needed to reject, if only to justify his own activities and thus save his own soul. In the bed of justice, Sterne allows Elizabeth Shandy to suggest attitudes that complicate almost every aspect of human sexuality; that she does so primarily by repeating Walter's comments, adding only minimally to the verbal clutter of Shandy Hall, is the most poignant of the many ironies of the chapter.

Walter's primary aim in the discussion is not to get Tristram into breeches, but to regain possession of that "otherness" which is his wife. This is a Sunday night bed of justice, and Walter has—presumably—finished his monthly "duty"; as always, the encounter with the *other* produces in him that irritable desire to establish priority and superiority, which is his most salient characteristic. No place is less conducive to this aim, however, than the Shandy marriage bed. The unity Walter seeks with another is total subordination, the triumph of self even within the marital embrace. His perfect *other*, the perfect "mate," is a person who would echo his own words, whose otherness would totally disappear, so coincident would be their lives and opinions. His perfect partner is himself.

Elizabeth echoes his words, but in doing so she creates ironic distances that lead us to understand each repetition as a separation and distinction; she is, in brief, a splendid satirist who has taken the full measure of Walter Shandy. In responding as he seems to require, she exhibits the fallacy of his idea of possession. His grasp continually slips, as it does on all his theories, and on the world they have tried to contain. The fertility of Mrs. Shandy's repetitions overwhelms the sterile agreement Walter has hoped to produce. Here is the most telling such moment:

> But indeed he is growing a very tall lad,—rejoin'd my father.
> ——He is very tall for his age, indeed,—said my mother.——
> ——I can not (making two syllables of it) imagine, quoth my father, who the duce he takes after.——
> I cannot conceive, for my life,—said my mother.———
> Humph!——said my father. (VI.38.437/526–27)

The many hints of illegitimacy hovering over Tristram's head culminate in this exchange, although Elizabeth does no more than repeat Walter's assertions. Between his acknowledgment of Tristram's height and her agreement, however, a vast abyss opens, into which all Walter's doubts and anxieties, prejudices and fears, are allowed to plunge. While previously we might have thought Walter's sexual anxiety had to do with performance, it is here made clear that possession is uppermost in his mind. But as Sterne demonstrates in his discussion of the legal settlement in the case of the Duke of Norfolk (IV.29), the origin of this anxiety is not in morality, but in property. We are not reading a social drama in which the wife's possible adultery is a moral or even familial concern, but a satiric narrative in which, I would argue, the entire world commits adultery, constantly *betraying* Walter's need for total possession, total control.

Almost every male character in *Tristram Shandy* has been suspected, at one time or another, of fathering Tristram, including Toby,

Yorick, and even—good grief—Dr. Slop! Interestingly, however, even the most thoroughgoing such examination[9] omits my own favorite candidate. The famous painter William Hogarth provided two illustrations for *Tristram Shandy*. The first, which we know Sterne specifically requested, is of the reading of the sermon and features four male characters, Walter, Toby, Trim, and Dr. Slop. The second, accompanying the publication of volumes III and IV in late 1760, illustrates the christening scene in IV.14; in the very center, holding the infant Tristram in his arms, stands a character who appears *only* in this chapter, and once more in the work (VI. 7)—the curate named Tristram, who insists that Susannah's *"Tristram-gistus"* is an error and, therefore, gives Tristram his own name, the primary "fathering" act from a legal standpoint. If we can surmise that Sterne discussed with Hogarth the scene he wanted for this illustration, as he had done for the first, is the use of Hogarth's pen to give us a picture of this curate an extraordinary, extratextual clue, one beyond Tristram's own words, one, in a sense, beyond the Shandys' control?

Frankly, I doubt it. No son was ever, to my mind, more like his father than Tristram is like Walter, and the curate in the illustration is the same height as Walter; had Sterne in mind the scenario I am writing, I assume he would have had Hogarth draw a taller figure. But this is to argue like Walter, claim and counterclaim. Mrs. Shandy is far more effective, separating herself from both her husband's possessiveness and my "penetrating" criticism by demonstrating that Tristram's creation is the result of sexuality, not legality, and that we must resist the temptation to argue ourselves into certainty about his—or any other—life and opinion. Rather, we must learn to take pleasure in the abyss that opens somewhere between the assertion and the agreement that Tristram is tall, in the mystery created by the curate's curious appearance (like Don Diego in Strasbourg) at midnight in Shandy Hall, to give his own name to the child. Mrs. Shandy turns the point directly on Walter:

> ——But don't you think it right? added my father, pressing the point home to her.
> Perfectly, said my mother, if it pleases you, Mr. *Shandy*.——

Joy

——There's for you! cried my father, losing temper——
Pleases me!——You never will distinguish, Mrs. *Shandy* . . .
betwixt a point of pleasure and a point of convenience.——This
was on the *Sunday* night;——and further this chapter sayeth not.
(VI.28.438–39/529)

The "point" is almost certainly sexual, but at the very moment of
"pressing" it "home" (a domesticating image), Walter strives to preserve his own sense of self at the expense of his partner.

The distinction between pleasure and convenience echoes the
earlier dichotomies that introduced the bed of justice, "vigour" versus
"discretion," "spirit" versus "sobriety"; together, these pairings suggest, above all, the moral turn given to human sexuality by Christian
dogmatics. The imposition of "duty" returns sexual activity to one's
own concerns and, ultimately, one's own salvation—the final concern.
In so far as the notion of "pleasure" suggests moral weakness, a culpable indulgence of appetite, one separates oneself from the partner, the
other, who experiences it, rejecting the otherness that may be our only
access to self-understanding and self-fulfillment, the "joy of sex." It is
a telling confirmation of Sterne's insight—and a telling condemnation
of our own so called sexual freedom—that today we need psychia-
trists, manuals, and talk shows to instruct us that these two words, *joy*
and *sex,* just might have something to do with one another.

During this discussion of the women of Shandy Hall, we need to
keep in mind that the "rules" governing human sexual activity in
Western society evolved in paternalistic settings, that is, in societies in
which males had a seemingly inalienable right to authority and property, and females did not. Sterne's own awareness of this male bias
appears in one of the very first documents incorporated into the work,
the lying-in article of the "marriage settlement" (I.15), which is provided with all the exuberance of parody, and yet hardly exaggerates
actual legal documents. Here, and again in a second instance of legal
satire, the Visitation dinner, the intimate connection between sexuality
and the law is made clear; the activities of the woman must be totally
controlled, totally within the power of the male, so that the father's
role if a birth occurred could be attested. The fertile repetitions of

Mrs. Shandy in the bed of justice become, in these legal treatises, the sterile redundancies of the law: "doth grant, covenant, condescend, consent, conclude, bargain, and fully agree to and with . . ." or again, "without any let, suit, trouble, disturbance, molestation, discharge, hinderance, forfeiture, eviction, vexation, interruption, or incumberance whatsoever" (I.15.38–39/43–44). As had many writers before him, Sterne has fun with the most salient feature of legalistic writing, its desire to construct a single sentence from which there can be no evasion or escape.

Within the legal demands of marriage, the various restrictions and limitations serve one end, the husband's sole "possession" of the wife. One talks a good deal about women as "property" in an abstract sense, but here the meaning is quite literal: a husband "owned" his wife solely in the interest of preventing trespass; he "owned" his daughters for the same reason. In the marriage article Sterne invents, Mrs. Shandy is allowed again to act "at her own will and pleasure . . . as if she was a *femme sole* [single woman] and unmarried" (I.15.39/44–45), but only when she is already pregnant. Nothing could be more suggestive of Sterne's insight into chastity's origin in legal inheritance than this; unable to conceive because she is already pregnant, the woman is finally released to her pleasure, given back to her "self"; that Elizabeth Shandy may have proposed the article is greatly to her credit; perhaps she suspected what marriage to Walter Shandy would entail.

More to the point, Sterne allows the women of *Tristram Shandy* to reject, along with other male notions of possession and power, authority and control, the notion of chastity. The women manifest a wonderful frankness about their sexuality, but Sterne's point must surely be balanced against the equally wonderful sexual reticence of the Shandy males. What seems to take place is yet another chiasmus, a crossing over, whereby the sexual laws imposed by men on women (For their own good, to be sure!), are turned on the men themselves, rendering them inadequate, impotent, duty-bound, and, as the widow Wadman discovers, unable or unwilling to acknowledge sexual appetite. And, conversely, the sexual privileges of freedom and promiscuity that men reserved for themselves within the legal framework are now awarded to the women.

One might briefly compare *Tristram Shandy* in this respect to two other great fictions of the age, *Clarissa* (1747–48) and *Tom Jones* (1749), in both of which sexual chastity is a major theme. Tom must learn the social implications of promiscuity before becoming worthy of Sophia, who knows them without the need of experience, perhaps from birth. Although the high valuation of chastity seems to arise in the male fear of female appetite, the female is now assumed to have no appetite, to be perfectly and peacefully at one with the male need for her chastity. This contradiction is even more painful in Richardson, where the seducer is trapped by the lie inherent to eighteenth-century sexual politics: Clarissa's chastity must be surrendered to the very man for whom it is the sole mark of her marriageability. Sterne gives no sign anywhere of having read either work; nevertheless, by putting the Shandy household under the sign of the *"bend sinister"* (IV.25.314/ 373) and by creating women who, when the time is ripe, make no bones about kicking out the "corking pin" from their nightgowns (VIII.9), Sterne joins Richardson and Fielding in examining one of the commonplaces of sexual morality in a paternalistic age, the demand for female chastity.

In discussing the bed of justice, I concentrated on the legal construction of sexual relations, eliding for the moment certain religious (or moral) considerations that can now be brought into play. Eighteenth-century Christianity not only agreed with the law on the issue of chastity, but was its chief mainstay and—until the century's end—its primary enforcer. As part of his clerical duties, Sterne himself sat as a judge during the semiannual assizes, or church courts, which had jurisdiction over such "crimes" as fornication, promiscuity, and adultery.[10] He would have been expected to punish them all, although his sermons largely stay clear of the subject—a bit of prudence on Sterne's part in that there were probably few secrets in his small village parish. We ought not simply condemn the Church for paternalistic hypocrisy, bigotry, or repressive notions. Setting aside venereal disease and the communal burden of unwed mothers and their offspring, a strong case can be mounted, surely, for a sexual loyalty that has little to do with inheritance or property, much to do with care, honor, (self-) respect, kindness, dedication, and good faith. Or, conversely, a case might be made to demonstrate the inaneness of sexual promiscuity, the unending search for a perfection not humanly possible, a variety that devours itself with its own sameness. What is perhaps the most interesting aspect of Sterne's inquiry into human sexuality is that it offers no inducement to licentiousness, no prod to appetite. Within the *spirit* of Christianity (if not the *letter*), Sterne found a means of dealing with appetite that satisfied his moral as well as physical nature.

As early as 1760, Sterne promises us that the courtship between Toby and the widow Wadman would be the "choicest morsel" of his work (IV.32.337/401), a suggestion that whatever else *Tristram* would deal with, it would eventually come to the subject of love, about which Tristram warns us: "when I do get at 'em [the amours]—assure yourselves, good folks,—(nor do I value whose squeamish stomach takes offence at it) I shall not be at all nice in the choice of my words. . . ." Sterne is following this plan when, at the end of volume V, he reduces Walter's intellectual pretensions to the theory of auxiliary verbs, and, in the middle of volume VI, closes down Toby's bowling green. The stage, in his own image, is ready for the courtship to begin, and volume six rushes the story forward; Sterne's awareness of his narrative line is indicated by the diagrams of his progress in chapter 40.

But at this point, in the winter of 1761–62, Sterne's health failed and he sought renewal in France. His wife and daughter accompanied him during some, but not all, of these travels; when he returned to London in 1764, he was alone. During the intervening years he had made little progress on *Tristram Shandy*, although probably more than he wanted to admit. That is to say, I suspect he had much of volume VIII written, perhaps even some of volume IX; the story of Toby and the widow could be written in a straight line at any time, because he knew almost precisely where he was going—toward a final climactic scene in which the real reason for the widow's interest in Toby's groin is revealed to him. But *Tristram Shandy* is a work, as Sterne well knew, that was not to be shaped as a narrative, a sequential story; unless he could disrupt the telling of the amours as much as he had disrupted the birthing of Tristram in the first six volumes, he would not be writing what he had set out to write—a satire of all that he found "Laugh-at-able."[11] His dilemma was solved with the discovery that his travels could be turned to use. Within the year, the heteroclite volume VII was at the printers.

Tristram's race against death has as its goal, we may assume, continued life, projected primarily in the figure of women. Invoking them, Tristram prays for the creative energy that can keep his book and his days continuous and endless. Hence, as we follow him through France, we find ourselves on a sexual quest: "Ah! ma chere fille! said I, as she tripp'd by, from her matins—you look as rosy as the morning (for the sun was rising, and it made the compliment the more gracious) . . ." (VII.7.487/585). The scene reminds us by vivid contrast of Tristram's ill health; certainly part of what Sterne sees in the "otherness" of women is the bodily health he has lost. The moment, however, goes no further than the compliment; the girl passes, Tristram moves on. A few chapters later, in Montreuil, he confronts Janatone, who "does the little coquetries very well," in much the same way: "A slut! in running them over within these five minutes that I have stood looking at her, she has let fall at least a dozen loops in a white thread stocking——Yes, yes—I see, you cunning gipsy!—'tis long, and taper . . ." (VII. 9.489–90/588–89). Here the portrait is more detailed, the invitation more forthright, but again the relationship is dropped before it begins. Tristram distances himself from appetite by playing the artist, but when he begins to measure a church instead of Janatone, he comes to a dramatic realization of the appetite she represents—the appetite for instability and change: "thou carriest the principles of change within thy frame." This recognition is placed, significantly, not in the context of a sexual appetite for variety, but of religious instability ("if the belief in Christ continues so long") and the procreative urge ("thou mayest grow out like a pumkin, and lose thy shapes . . . nay, thou mayest go off like a hussy—and lose thyself" [490/589–90]). A comparison is drawn to the indomitable absent heroine of *Tristram Shandy*, Aunt Dinah, and we are left with the impression that it is more valuable to measure Janatone than a church on one's travels—or pilgrimage.

The two encounters provide an important context for one of Tristram's most famous sentences, in chapter 13, comparing Bishop Hall's strictures against travel with his own enjoyments; his allusion to health and the evocation of joy are noteworthy: "Now, I (being very thin) think differently; and that so much of motion, is so much of life, and so much of joy——and that to stand still, or get on but slowly, is death and the devil——" (VII.13.493/593). Tristram invokes Jenny at this point, in the context of a mock acceptance of platonism (*"getting out of the body, in order to think well"*); and of a more serious counterargument, one that acknowledges the inescapable influence of the body on the mind: "REASON, is half of it, SENSE; and the measure of heaven itself is but the measure of our present appetites and concoctions——" (494/593). We need to understand that Sterne's dichotomy here is not between head and heart, reason and sentiment (or feeling), as it is so often taken to be. The difference between Tristram (Sterne, too, at this point) and the Bishop is that one is corpulent and the other thin and this bodily condition affects their "reasons"; between the Pythagoreans and Jenny, that the philosophers pretend to leave the *body* behind in order to think, while she, presumably, does not. Once again, Sterne chooses a religious icon, "heaven," as part of his argument. Since we can never leave our bodies (except through the deceptions of philosophers and other moralists), the *measure* of heaven suggested by Janatone and Jenny seems more valid than whatever the Pythagoreans have to offer; as had happened earlier, classical philosophy is found wanting when measured against Sterne's notions of reality.

In the next chapter, Sterne corrects our too rampant imaginations—his own included. On the one hand, the hell defined by the philosophers (quoted from Burton's *Anatomy of Melancholy*) is hardly more real than their heaven; on the other hand, the quick juxtaposition of invocations of heaven and hell suggests that Sterne's brush with death, his continuing illness, leaves him unable to explore sexuality without exploring as well his impending relationship with the divine. A dying Christian focuses on the "four last things": Death, Judgment, Heaven, and Hell. Hence, the heaven we are perhaps prone to erect from our encounter with Janatone and Jenny also will not do. The

Joy

notion of Christianity's decline within the next 50 years is again raised; two such passages within 10 pages is surely a deliberate reverberation (VII.9.490/589 and VII.14.495/595), but just as surely Sterne is not celebrating or advocating the demise of the Christian faith he seriously preached throughout his adult life—whatever Tristram might seem to suggest. Rather Sterne gropes—through Tristram's encounters and evasions—toward some attitude within the Christian communion that can distinguish between the bodily passions he has experienced (and continues to experience, despite—or because of—his diminishing health and vigor), and a licentiousness he knows he must reject: "Blessed Jupiter! and blessed every other heathen god and goddess! for now [with Christianity's demise] ye will all come into play again, and with Priapus at your tails——what jovial times!——but where am I? and into what a delicious riot of things am I rushing? I——I who must be cut short in the midst of my days, and taste no more of 'em than what I borrow from my imagination" (VII.14.495/595). The knotting together of death and sexuality that we see here is a dominant motif of the final three volumes of *Tristram Shandy*. The appetites of the body, properly acknowledged, and distinct from those of mind and heart, become the key to salvation.

Can human sexuality be a source of joy rather than shame, of grace rather than damnation, of fertility and creativeness rather than demonic marks of illness and impotence? While formulating these positives—joy, grace, creativeness—as abstract (Platonic) ideas is easy, Sterne returns always to an unashamed and frank physicality. If Priapian worship is rejected, so are Pythagoras and Plato, and even more, St. Paul and the Christian sanction of a cool and dutiful sexual act, such as Walter (dutifully) performs to the disappointment of Elizabeth, and Toby recites to the equally disappointed widow Wadman (IX.25). What remains is not easy to define, but Sterne, much like Nietzsche, seeks his answers in the ironic spaces he perceives between our bodies and our language—or, in Tristram's terms, between our lives and our opinions.

It is within this space that one may justify the hyperextended story of the abbess of Andoüillets. Given the convent's repressiveness, sexuality still finds two outlets. One depends on a transparency of language, which, through repetition (as in responsive readings of Scripture, one might note), seems to produce real bodily presence. The nuns are moved, penetrated, by their divided words, much to their covert pleasure; a bodily man could not, perhaps, produce more. The second outlet depends on language's opacity, and results in a flirtation with perversities that brings the body back into play, but in darkly mysterious (and, ultimately, undefined) ways. Hence, the young novice has a "whitloe" or "white swelling" on her middle finger, brought about "by sticking it constantly into the abbess's cast poultices, &c." (VII.21.505/607). Any reader who has traveled this far into *Tristram Shandy* is bound to be wary of anything finger-shaped being stuck into anything of any shape. That suspicion is rendered far more certain by the *et cetera*, a traditional euphemism for the female pudenda; furthermore, *white swelling* was used to describe a pregnant woman. Somehow or another, the novice has gotten pregnant by sticking her finger into the abbess's *et cetera*— perversity disappears into incoherence, as it often does in *Tristram Shandy*, but only after allowing us to sample the confusions and disharmonies that result from the suppression of bodily appetites.

This disharmony is most often projected in the Shandy household as impotence or similar sexual inadequacy (a wound on the groin, a window-sash circumcision, a short nose); hence, we are prepared to read the following passage as almost certainly Tristram's confession of a bout with impotence:

> ——Do, my dear Jenny, tell the world for me, how I behaved under one [disaster], the most oppressive of its kind which could befall me as a man, proud, as he ought to be, of his manhood——
> 'Tis enough, said'st thou, coming close up to me, as I stood with my garters in my hand, reflecting upon what had *not* pass'd——'Tis enough, Tristram, and I am satisfied, said'st thou, whispering these words in my ear, **** ** **** *** ******;— **** ** ****——any other man would have sunk down to the center——(VII.29.517–18/624)

What is of interest here, in addition to Tristram's belief that goat's milk will restore not only potency but add seven years to his life (thus reinforcing the connection between sexuality and mortality), is the fact that we cannot decipher Tristram's asterisks. We recall that when Susannah asks the young Tristram to "**** *** ** *** ******," we had no similar difficulty (V.17.376/ 449). Here, however, Jenny's words disengage themselves from Tristram's text (from any readable representation in the text), all but these: "'Tis enough, Tristram, and I am satisfied. . . ." What other words could possibly follow this tender acceptance of human weakness and human failure, along with Jenny's frank acknowledgment that the end of sexuality is pleasure (satisfaction)?

Jenny does not attempt to restore Tristram's "manhood"; rather, she asserts her own "womanhood," the pleasure she sought and found with him. Her capacity to remain fully her own subject, while not forgetting the subject before her, "garters in hand," is the mystery of human sexuality, of love, that Sterne has tried to elucidate. Jenny's frank acknowledgment of her own body is an invitation into this mystery, but Tristram, with a gesture to be repeated at the end of the volume, masks desire behind censorial asterisks, much as the nuns of Andoüillets had masked their desires, refusing to speak those "words magic!" (VII.24.508/612). One might even suggest that Jenny has whispered to Tristram the secret of a physical love acceptable to God; however, where "any other man" hearing her words might have penetrated to the heart (the center) of the mystery, Tristram "dances" away, seeking love and life in Wales (and goat's milk). This is the moment of Tristram's greatest impotence, and it is reflected by our own impotence, as we stand, vocabularies in hand, confronting a sentence of divided asterisks that we cannot decode (penetrate).

The last adventure of volume VII might well have been the one Tristram has all along been seeking. Nannette, with the "cursed slit" in her petticoat, invites him to the dance and to a great deal more. Once again, a Shandy male flees from the frank avowal of female sexual appetite: "*Viva la joia!* was in her lips—*Viva la joia!* was in her eyes. A transient spark of amity shot across the space betwixt us——She look'd amiable! . . . Just disposer of our joys and sorrows, cried I, why could not a man sit down in the lap of content here—and dance, and sing, and say his prayers, and go to heaven with this nut brown maid? capriciously did she bend her head on one side, and dance up insiduous—— Then 'tis time to dance off, quoth I . . ." (VII.43.538/651).

Nannette embodies all the women of the Shandy world, and Tristram's response is that of the Shandy men (excluding, of course, Trim). Certainly, we can impose our morality on the scene, the laws of marriage, the errors of promiscuity, and on and on. We can also impose our realities on the scene, puncture the pastoral fantasy, despise the Eve-as-vamp stereotype, and scorn the bourgeois male's desire for "nut brown maids" as a reactionary nostalgia to play the landlord. But our morality and our reality do little damage to Sterne's loving picture, in part because he anticipates our morality (sadly enough) by having Tristram flee the scene, in part because we are imposing flawed patriarchal judgments on Nannette ("good girls don't have slits in their petticoats"). Sterne, on the contrary, seems quite willing, following the lead of Mrs. Shandy and the widow Wadman, to allow Nannette her own mode of expression, even if it tempts the body quite powerfully to surrender to appetite. Sterne appears to have been often tempted to sexual engagements that promised joy in the lips, the eyes, in every part; what he has sought throughout the work, and in Tristram's mad dash in this volume, is a better understanding of that temptation. As Tristram dances away, we glimpse the importance of separating Sterne from his unreliable narrator; the Sterne who was writing *Tristram Shandy* in 1765, ill and alone, and more and more convinced that the body was as much an instrument of God's grace as the mind and the heart, would not, I believe, have danced away.

That Sterne is now closer to the understanding he seeks, involving not only men's relationship to women, but the human relationship to God, is suggested in the last two scenes I discuss in this chapter. The first occurs in chapter 8 of the final volume and is one of his most beautiful passages, one in which we finally hear the authentic voice of Sterne, rather than the masking voice of Tristram. Once again, the invocation of Jenny is vital for our understanding of the passage, for her responsive kindness in the "impotence" scene, accompanied by her understanding of her own needs and desires and their satisfaction, make her the fit audience for Tristram's confession of what we have increasingly suspected was driving him (and Sterne) as both writers and seekers:

Joy

I will not argue the matter: Time wastes too fast: every letter I trace tells me with what rapidity Life follows my pen; the days and hours of it, more precious, my dear Jenny! than the rubies about thy neck, are flying over our heads like light clouds of a windy day, never to return more——every thing presses on—— whilst thou art twisting that lock,——see! it grows grey; and every time I kiss thy hand to bid adieu, and every absence which follows it, are preludes to that eternal separation which we are shortly to make.——

——Heaven have mercy upon us both! (IX.8.610– 11/754)

The reader who can fully grasp why the pain and longing chronicled in this passage is a carefully crafted reflection of Nannette and the "cursed slit" in her petticoat (Nannette and Jenny coalescing to represent all the women of the work), has found an important clue to the endurance of the best authors: they inevitably speak to the deepest shared concerns of our everyday life, those events we *must* think about when we can no longer distract ourselves with intellectual pretensions, abstract vocabularies, and philosophical games, that is, with our hobby-horses. Love and death are clearly two such concerns, and *Tristram Shandy* is a meditation on both.

In *A Sentimental Journey*, Sterne returns once more to Nannette, although not by name. In the penultimate chapter of everything Sterne ever wrote, Yorick finds a moment of communion in a peasant dance, much as had Tristram at the end of volume VII. Nothing interferes this time, however, with Yorick's appreciation of the moment. In harmony with himself, he is able to be in harmony with others—with the *other*. The beautiful assertion that he beholds "*Religion* mixing in the dance" (*Journey*, 284) is an insight he (and Sterne) have gained from travel and loneliness and, as already suggested, the impending threat of death, which renders the need for human connection all the more intense and necessary—and yet, in view of divine judgment, all the more threatening. Sterne revisits the scene in order to acknowledge, one last time, a God he has found who does not flinch at the human need for others, who comprehends the appetite that renders nut brown maids or swains worthy objects of desire, not inferior to objects of more pretended worth—namely, objects not of the body, but of the heart and mind, the "virtues" of piety and chastity, decorum and moderation, by which we try to lead a life that *puts the body in its proper place*. Sterne's chapter title, "Grace," confirms the notion of a divine blessing on this appetite (significantly, the dance is a "grace" after supper); the fall from Grace is not the dance of the body, but the dance away from it.

The scene echoes not only Nannette's dance in *Tristram Shandy*, but the festivity pictured in Sterne's sermon on the return of the prodigal son, where we are told that "When the affections so kindly break loose, Joy, is another name for Religion" (*Sermons* [1766], III:147). Together, the three texts suggest Sterne's own sense of a return to Grace after much wandering, a return to Joy after much fear and much sadness. Above all, they offer a promise of salvation, despite, or because of, his honest confrontation with the appetites and desires of his own body. Sterne's Grace-giving God appears to be the very same one Nietzsche's nonbelieving Zarathustra insists on:

"I should believe only in a God who understood how to dance."[12]

9

Tartuffery

Character	*Sterne*
Foil	*Myself*
Incident	*The "Whiskers Chapter"*
Document	*Nietzsche's "The Most Liberated Writer"*
Activity	*Reading*
Image	*The Blank Page*
-Ism	*Skepticism*

Philology is to be understood here in a very wide sense as the art of reading well—of being able to read off a fact *without* falsifying it by interpretation, *without* losing caution, patience, subtlety in the desire for understanding. Philology as *ephexis* [undecisiveness] in interpretation.

(*Twilight*, 169)

Nietzsche's formulation for reading well is a natural outgrowth of the classical skepticism that permeates his philosophy—and much post-modernist critical thinking as well. Insofar as reading becomes a public act primarily through writing, the two are intimately entwined. Thus, when Nietzsche reads Sterne as a writer of "endless melody," in whom "the fixed form is constantly being broken up, displaced, transposed back into indefiniteness, so that it signifies one thing and at the same time another" (*Human*, 238), we may think of Sterne as a model for Nietzsche's "good" reader, one able to suspend belief in the very process of interpreting or understanding the world; his book, *Tristram Shandy*, is the written expression of that capacity to read well. Or, not quite conversely, we may think of Nietzsche exhibiting in his evaluation of Sterne precisely the qualities of the good reader he has praised: he assigns to Sterne what is really his own most desired aesthetic attribute, an "endless melody." Thus, if Nietzsche is right about reading well, he has created a critical impasse reflective of the skeptic's dilemma: in the ideal dance between writer and reader, world and observer, self and other, we cannot tell with certainty the dancer from the dance.

Nietzsche's criticism of Sterne appears among the "Assorted Opinions and Maxims" that comprise the second part of *Human, All Too Human* (1886); although I have quoted an extensive portion in chapter 3, I do so again because we are now in a better position to analyze what Nietzsche intended when he called Sterne "The most liberated writer": "How, in a book for free spirits, should there be no mention of Laurence Sterne, whom Goethe honoured as the most liberated spirit of his century! Let us content ourselves here simply with calling him the most liberated spirit of all time, in comparison with whom all others seem stiff, square, intolerant and boorishly direct" (*Human*, 238). What is most interesting about Nietzsche's praise in these opening sentences is its magnificent, defiant, *decisiveness*. As is usually the case, Nietzsche's rhetoric is artful: the invocation of Goethe, for example, ensures agreement from his readers, while, by taking the praise even further, from "of his century" to "of all time," Nietzsche suggests he can better Goethe's judgment. He is also aware that Germans would tend to reserve the title "most liberated spirit" for Goethe alone; indeed Goethe's application of the epithet to Sterne is probably our best indication of how Goethe wanted *himself* to be eulogized. And this is also true for Nietzsche; the subtitle of *Human, All Too Human* is "A Book for Free Spirits" and in all of Nietzsche's writings, his need to separate himself from stiff and intolerant ideologies is paramount. The great irony of Nietzsche's canon is that this liberal spirit speaks so often with the thunderous voice of prophecy, the essence of which is positiveness, decisiveness, and certainty.

It is this irony, I believe, that Nietzsche found at the heart of Sterne's writing—precisely because he recognized it as his own core: "for he knows how to encompass both [laughing and seriousness] in a *single* facial expression; he likewise knows how, and even wants to be in the right and in the wrong at the same time, to knot together profundity and farce." Again, one confronts the basic dilemma (and joy) of skepticism: being right about anything necessitates a wrongness within one's own system of belief; the profoundest insight we can have is that our depth in no way has brought us closer to the truth, has indeed, driven us away from it—Swift's governing insight in *A Tale of a Tub*.

For Nietzsche, the essential moral act is to confront the dilemma without dogmatism and without despair (or what Thomas Mann astutely labels "mystic community" and "windy individualism"). Again, Sterne is found to be a Nietzschean overcomer. He eschews dogmatism with his "irony towards all sententiousness" (and this compliment comes from perhaps the greatest producer of sententious maxims since Samuel Johnson); and he eschews despair with his "antipathy to seriousness." But these are relatively minor talents, shared by many; Sterne's genius (Nietzsche's genius) is to hold these talents in brilliant tension with "a tendency to be unable to regard anything merely superficially." To know that the truth will constantly elude us, but be unable or unwilling to lighten the burden of truth-seeking—this is the impossible task Nietzsche sets for the reader: Sterne "produces in the right reader a feeling of uncertainty as to whether one is walking, standing or lying: a feeling, that is, closely related to floating" (*Human*, 239). We should not be deceived: we live by the laws of gravity, and "floating" is as impossible to our minds as to our bodies. The instinct when one is cut loose from gravity is to right oneself, to reanchor oneself in certainty; the metaphor tells us much about the processes of reading and writing, and about Sterne's complex achievement.

Nietzsche is also aware that one of Sterne's (and his own) primary secrets is reversal of roles: "He, the supplest of authors, communi-
cates something of this suppleness to his reader. Indeed, Sterne
unintentionally reverses these roles, and is sometimes as much reader
as author; his book resembles a play within a play, an audience
observed by another audience" (*Human*, 239). Nietzsche describes
here his own vaunted "psychology," his belief that he is constantly on
the underside of the masks of human self-deception. In *Tristram
Shandy*, the attempt to place Sterne in Yorick or in Tristram is simply
the beginning of the problem of unmasking; by the end, it may occur
to us that it is never Sterne who is aligned with his characters, but only
readers who, as Sir or Madam Critick (II.2.85/97), assume the role of
writers and find in a foil—whether Yorick or Tristram or Locke or
Nietzsche or Bakhtin—a reading of *Tristram Shandy* congenial to their
own understanding. Sterne, a reader himself, aligns himself, as a
writer, sometimes with Yorick, sometimes with Tristram, sometimes
with Rabelais or Cervantes or Locke or Montaigne—and often enough
with yet another entity, who tries, desperately enough, to defy gravity
by hovering, floating among all possible roles.

Hence, to consider in this chapter the *character* as Sterne and his
foil as myself entails numerous roles on both sides of the equation.
Above all, it suggests that the phrase "Sterne means" or its equivalent,
is not only shorthand for "Sterne means to me," but for a more complicated equation in which the pretense of a solution to *Tristram
Shandy* (that is, what it *means*) confronts our inability even to fix the
primary roles of the interpretative drama, that of protagonist (writer)
and foil (reader). Without doubt, this is a fundamental problem in all
interpretative acts, but more commonplace writers exert their energies
in the direction of defining both roles; as writers, they create the readers they want by seeming to come to rest in the certainties or fixities
that impel their writing. Sterne, to the contrary, compounds the problem, as Nietzsche realized, by trying very hard to mean contradictory
things, to keep his text floating above (or below) certainties. Is it possible, then, for us to read *Tristram Shandy*—or any text? In this final
chapter, I want to examine the implications of this question, keeping
Nietzsche's closing remarks on Sterne in mind: "That which good

Tartuffery

French writers, and before them certain Greeks and Romans, wanted and were able to do in prose is precisely the opposite of what Sterne wants and is able to do: for, as the masterly exception, he raises himself above that which all artists demand of themselves: discipline, compactness, simplicity, restraint in motion and deportment" (*Human*, 239). Nietzsche goes on from this observation to condemn Sterne's personal life (which he knew only from censorious nineteenth-century biographical accounts), his "squirrel-soul" that leaped restlessly from branch to branch, and his "shamelessly watering eyes and play of sensibility on his features."

It is worth repeating my earlier observation that Nietzsche is reading himself in reading Sterne, and thus even his condemnation of Sterne's "baroque, indeed depraved imagination" seems to echo Nietzsche's own sadly inaccurate sense of himself, along with his pathological fear of self-deception. Similarly, a particularly Nietzschean irony is found in his suggestion that Sterne triumphed over "discipline," "compactness," and other classical virtues, virtues that "*all* artists demand of themselves" (emphasis mine). The pose of the unrestrained writer is common to both authors, but the creation of ambiguity, of a constantly hovering or floating text, against all the laws of gravity (and the human urge toward certainty), requires the most consummate discipline—and both Sterne and Nietzsche are majestically *disciplined* in imagination and self-consciously *compact* (that is, aphoristic) in style.

Had Sterne stopped short with an irony directed at sententiousness, an antipathy toward seriousness, we might be justified in celebrating his denial of discipline, compactness, simplicity, and restraint. But such writers and readers without discipline are Nietzsche's archfoes, for they have stopped measuring and evaluating and judging. They have, in brief, failed the greatest test of philosophy, the "tendency to be unable to regard anything merely superficially." Significantly, Rousseau, a writer compared to Sterne by those interested in Sterne's "romanticism," is one of Nietzsche's favorite targets in this regard.[1] While his quarrel with Rousseau seems largely political, I suspect a more fundamental motive has to do with "soul-searching." Although all three may be said to have probed themselves intensely, Rousseau's emphasis is always on the constancy of his soul, while Nietzsche and Sterne probe "squirrel souls," their restless, ever-moving spirit of inquiry, fueled by self-condemnation and a fear of self-deception, which denies them equally the comforts of the surface or the solutions of the internal: "Last week I saw a woman *flayed*, and you will hardly believe how much it altered her person for the worse" is the way Swift dramatizes the plight of the skeptical mind in *A Tale of a Tub* (84).

In an earlier essay of mine, "Proust's Influence on Sterne: Remembrance of Things to Come," I explain the notion that a twentieth-century author can influence an eighteenth-century one with this observation: "twentieth-century readers, reading the best that has been produced in their own century, come to earlier literature through that experience and cannot free their reading from it."[2] Our reading, not only of literature but of our entire twentieth-century world, has been heavily influenced by Friedrich Nietzsche. It is also worth considering, however, in my own very particular case, as someone who has recently reread Nietzsche after a quarter century of scholarly concentration on Sterne, that I have been reading Nietzsche within a "Shandean" atmosphere. This circularity is vital in remapping the interplay between reader and writer that Nietzsche suggests is the key to Sterne's "suppleness." It is also a key to the reader's and writer's capacity to hover skeptically over the possibilities of interpretative certainty.

In reading Nietzsche through my version of Sterne's eyes, I find myself isolating and demarcating certain ideas as more important— more central—than others; this would seem to be the common strategy of all interpretative reading. Thus, my concentration on Nietzsche's scattered attacks on the "spirit of Gravity" and systems is predetermined by my prior reading of *Tristram Shandy*; on the other hand, my discovery of similar "themes" in *Tristram* is equally a symptom of my twentieth-century existence and, hence, of Nietzsche's influence. After all, I am no longer interested in isolating, to give one example, the "moral outrages" of Sterne, as were so many nineteenth-century critics—*Tartuffes*, as both Sterne and Nietzsche label those who fail to negotiate to their satisfaction the problems of reading and writing.

Tartuffery

Tartuffe is the hypocritical villain of Molière's play (first produced in 1664), who uses a mask of religious conviction to conceal his numerous vices, particularly lust and avarice. In *A Sentimental Journey*, Sterne has a French officer explain to Yorick that the tradition of a theater audience's shouting, "*Haussez les mains*" ("Up with your hands"), when a clergyman is seated next to a young woman, is an "illiberal sarcasm at the Church, which had begun in the theatre about the time the Tartuffe was given in it" (*Journey*, 180). The comment is particularly telling in view of two earlier references to Tartuffe in *Tristram Shandy*, the first in volume V, where Tristram leaves a bawdy chain of reasoning as a legacy to "Prudes and Tartufs" (V.1.343/ 408-9); and the second, in volume VIII, where tartuffery is tied to positiveness and certainty in all walks of life:

> . . . but I have no
> Zeal or Anger——or
> Anger or Zeal——
> And till gods and men agree together to call it by the same
> name——the errantest TARTUFFE, in science—in politics—or in
> religion, shall never kindle a spark within me. . . . (VIII.2.541/
> 657)

Throughout Nietzsche's writings, the figure of Tartuffe appears as the embodiment of attitudes to which he is opposed: he writes, for example, about "old Kant's tartuffery," the "inveterate Tartuffery of morality," and national "tartuffery" passing as national virtues in *Beyond Good and Evil*, while in *The Will to Power* he mentions the "tartuffery of idealism" and of "false scientific manners" (sections 311 and 424); those who, "with a touch of Tartuffe," base morality on the "*happiness of the greatest number*" (section 20); and the language of Otto von Bismarck (presumably) as "court-chaplain Tartuffery" (section 191). Too much is encompassed in these diverse usages to be reduced to a single concept, but this passage from *The Will to Power* seems to come close to Nietzsche's primary meaning of "tartuffery": "The demand for 'humanization' (which quite naïvely believes itself to possess the formula for 'what is human?') is a tartuffery, behind which a quite definite type of man seeks to attain domination: more exactly, a quite definite instinct, the herd instinct—'Human equality': behind which is concealed the tendency to make men more and more alike."[3] Several of Nietzsche's favorite themes come together here, but for our purposes—connection with Sterne's usage—his condemnation of those who believe they possess the truth (enthusiasts or zealots, in eighteenth-century terms), and his assumption that morality is a hypocritical mask for the will to power (domination) are the most important. We may return these broad implications to our more narrow scope by refocusing attention on the reader/writer relationship: a paraphrase might then suggest that the reader as Tartuffe is one who proposes to gain control of the text (and its author) by imposing on that author an understanding (interpretation) deemed universal despite its local origins. Tartuffery is censorship.

Sterne tweaks the reader's nose (Sir or Madam) on numerous occasions as censorious readers, but his most persistent Tartuffe was Bishop William Warburton (1698–1779), author of the monumental *Divine Legation of Moses* (1738–41), the editor of Pope's works, and, in the words of Edward Gibbon, "the Dictator and tyrant" of the literary world of mid-eighteenth-century England. Sterne's early intention almost certainly was to include Warburton as a character in *Tristram Shandy*, possibly as a tutor for Tristram. When, however, the word reached Warburton and his friends, some "friendly persuasion" brought Sterne to drop the plan. Warburton's response to the first two volumes was enthusiastic ("the English Rabelais," he perceptively noted), but he turned harshly critical in later years. Certainly the public rumor that he had "bought" his way out of *Tristram Shandy* must have rankled, but I have also argued elsewhere that from volume V onward, Sterne alludes to Warburton covertly on several different occasions, and always in a manner that the Bishop would recognize as an insult.[4]

That Warburton is on Sterne's mind is indicated by the mottoes on the title page of volume V, for they all respond to Warburton's advice to "curb" his wit as befits a clergyman, to laugh only as suits company where "priests and virgins may be present" (*Letters*, 119).[5] Sterne's mottoes respond:

Tartuffery

If I speak too lightly or freely, you will indulge this liberty.
If any quarrelsome persons should censure my jesting as either too light for a divine or too satirical for a decent Christian—not I, but Democritus said it.
If any priest or monk engages in jesting words, raising laughter, let him be damned.[6]

The first two sentences are from Horace and Erasmus, via Burton's *Anatomy of Melancholy*, and suggest, respectively, toleration and evasion; the third is from the Second Council of Carthage, in the early days of Christianity, and is clearly intolerant. Together, they represent a spectrum of attitudes that confront tartuffery without resolving it; Sterne's text, beginning with the very first chapter of volume V, creates the same irresolution.

In this chapter, Tristram pays back his promise of a chapter on whiskers, invoking "Prudes and Tartufs" as his witnesses. It is one of the most puzzling episodes of the work, for it appears to be gratuitous, an unnecessary repetition of what has already been demonstrated with *noses*—that is, that any word in the English language is susceptible to the imposition of a sexual denotation, given sufficient suggestion. Moreover, given the Warburtonian context, it appears almost a childish bit of effrontery on Sterne's part; not only will he insist on his bawdy, but will do so without even a feint toward justification (what today we call redeeming social or aesthetic value). Tristram's excuse for the content of the chapter is a lame but telling one: he had never seen the "underwritten fragment" before putting it into his book to fulfill his promise (343/409). The play of ideas results in a knot; do we expect writers to read their books before they write them? Or, having written them, not to read and excise that which should be "steered clear of?" Is Tristram acting the part of Nietzsche's philologist, exercising the utmost undecisiveness in reading (and writing) by refusing to erase or exclude anything? And is this refusal, especially in the face of tartuffery, a monumental commitment, a *decisive* engagement with any and all opposition?

In repeating the restlessness and divisions of Strasbourg, the kingdom of *Navarre* suggests once again the human need to define and comprehend the world. But where *nose* seemed so clearly to convert itself into the *phallus, whiskers* defies definition, primarily because this particular passage leads nowhere: "There is not a cavalier . . . that has so gallant a pair—Of what? cried *Margaret,* smiling—— Of whiskers, said *La Fosseuse,* with infinite modesty" (V.1.344/410). We are tempted, perhaps, to substitute *legs* since *pair of legs* is common enough, and we are allowed to hold that interpretation for several paragraphs. But then comes La Maronette's praise: "I never saw an officer of the horse-guards in my life . . . with two such legs" (V.1.345/411) and we immediately realize our reading was *wrong.* I deliberately stress this wrongness, because the idea of an indeterminate text is so often confused with a meaningless one. One of Sterne's shrewdest insights about language, however, is to recognize the vast difference between the two, despite what may be their shared basis in human weakness: as interpretative beings we are unable to establish certainty, but equally unable to rest without assigning meaning. Indeed, as we tease *meaning* from the fragment, just as the women of Navarre tease it from *whiskers,* we begin to exhibit the same division and restlessness, the interplay of pleasure, interpretation, and power that lies at the heart of reading.

Sterne's bawdy joke, "and for the women,——*they* were divided" (V.1.345/410) suggests to me the fecundity neither of indeterminacy nor meaninglessness, but of interpretation. One often reads in recent Sterne criticism about the fertile indeterminacy of the text. Sterne's text, however, is richly determined, although often under the banner of differing camps—and this, I suggest, is much closer to the experience of language and ideas in the marketplace than more theoretical notions suggesting the infinite *play* of language. *Nose, bridge,* and *crevice* are never cut free from meaning, never allowed to float detached from user and usage, never undetermined. That Toby *mistakes* Slop's "bridge" for a "bridge" on the bowling green is a humorous error precisely because we understand that Slop's "bridge" is a support for Tristram's nose; without that understanding, there is no joke.

We are also convinced that in this passage "bridge" is not the card game, and also that it does not mean "nose" (a "thrusting bridge," however, is a different matter). In that direction lies the sterility of Shandean theorizing or system-making, in which a "white bear," or Christian name, or any other militant reductiveness, is pressed to carry the entire burden of the human search for understanding. Sterne, to the contrary, locates human creativity and purpose in the division of interpretation, division among both readers and readings—not because division always offers a *third* "true" choice (the "middle way" of classical thought), but because it offers a *second*—an insistence on the *other*—as part of every interpretative act. Perhaps this is the reason that Sterne's "conversation" and "communication," and our "intercourse," all seek their meaning somewhere between the pleasures of dialogue and of sexual union.

Yet *whiskers* remains undefined, undefinable, and thus "ruined," "indecent," and "unfit for use." Sterne's citation at this point of the "curate *d'Estella*" only deepens the puzzle. The Florida editors cite a passage from a seventeenth-century work, Diego d'Estella's *Contempt of the World*, that may be apropos: "Amongst men that have had civil bringing up, it hath bene taken alwaies for a foule and a shamefull thing, to use dishonest & ribauld speeches, although they be spoken but in jest. How much more ought they then to be avoided amongst the servantes of God? Be circumspect in al thy wordes, let them be wel weighed and considered, before thou utter them. . . . Much evil growes of naughty words."[7] This is well within the tradition of the Second Council of Carthage some 1,500 years earlier and echoes in every way Warburton's advice; did Sterne have it or a similar passage in mind when he invoked d'Estella?

Or is it possible that he never read d'Estella, a Franciscan monk, at all? Interestingly, he used the name as a pseudonym as early as 1739–40 (perhaps punning on star = starling = starn = Sterne, the last part of which chain he calls attention to in *A Sentimental Journey* [205]); and a humorous (rather than literal) identification is indicated when we are told about d'Estella's warning about noses, which is, undoubtedly, a fiction. As with any attempt to tie Sterne to a particular voice, division occurs; the real d'Estella, as just quoted, seems to take the wrong side of the question from Sterne in defending self-censorship, but we have perhaps read more literalness into the name than was called for. The fictional d'Estella, on the other hand, seems to speak for Sterne, but his words are misunderstood by the world. In the conflict between the two, one might hear the "*extreams* of DELICACY, and the *beginnings* of CONCUPISCENCE," but as with *whiskers* themselves, it seems impossible to "read" the *fact* of d'Estella's presence in *Tristram Shandy* "*without* falsifying it by interpretation, *without* losing caution, patience, subtlety in the desire for understanding" (*Antichrist*, 169).

At the end of volume V, Sterne introduces a second clerical figure who echoes his struggles with Warburton and the questions of tartuffery we have been examining. Tristram explains his father's slow progress on the *Tristrapædia* by analogy to the unlikely figure of Giovanni della Casa, the sixteenth-century archbishop of Benevento, author of a famous Renaissance courtesy book, the *Galateo*. According to Tristram, della Casa believed that "whenever a Christian was writing a book . . . his first thoughts were always the temptations of the evil one." And when the writer was particularly noteworthy, a bishop, for example, then "all the devils in hell broke out of their holes to cajole him. . . . So that the life of a writer . . . was not so much a state of *composition*, as a state of *warfare*; and his probation in it, precisely that of any other man militant upon earth,—both depending alike, not half so much upon the degrees of his WIT—as his RESISTANCE" (V.16.374/447). Tristram's della Casa glories in the slightness, the enervation, of his work, "not of above half the size or the thickness of a *Rider*'s Almanack" (373/446), which means it had fewer than 10 small pages. He appears to be a precise embodiment of Nietzsche's litany of qualities Sterne is said to rise above: "discipline, compactness, simplicity, restraint in motion and deportment"; and his affirmation of the linkage between writing and warfare echoes the point I have made concerning the important similarity between Walter and Toby—as well as tying Warburton into the equation, whose opinion it was that the "state of Authorship, whatever that of Nature be, is certainly a state of war."[8] In addition, the typography of della Casa's WIT and RESISTANCE reflects d'Estella's DELICACY and CONCUPISCENCE, as, indeed, the two surnames echo each other.

Della Casa appears twice more in *Tristram*, the first time when Tristram draws his diagrams of progressive "improvement," and notes that the largest digression in volume V is the result of *"John de la Casse*'s devils" (VI.40). In order to proceed in the straight line he draws with the help of a "writing-master's ruler," he must have "the good leave of his grace of *Benevento*'s devils" (VI.40.474/571–72). In volume IX, della Casa appears in Tristram's discussion of "heterogeneous matter," the need to "keep up that just balance betwixt wisdom and folly, without which a book would not hold together a single year . . ." (IX.12.614/761). The remainder of this chapter and the next contain various mechanical operations of the spirit, artificial ways to induce wit sufficient to keep his work as heteroclite as he desires; the problem Tristram sets for himself is to forestall his story with digressions until the sixteenth chapter when he will be ready to begin again. Here Sterne winds the discussion back to della Casa, who, according to Tristram at this point, wrote a commentary on the Book of Revelation as penance for his *"nasty* Romance of the Galatea" (IX.14.618/765–66).

Sterne had learned from the margins of Rabelais or Burton that della Casa had written a celebration of sodomy, which he then confused with the *Galateo*, having obviously read neither. The error, like many similar errors and misdirections in *Tristram Shandy* (d'Estella comes appropriately to mind), is indicative of Sterne's desire to appear enormously learned. To write within the Rabelaisian–Cervantic–Burtonian–Swiftian tradition he had chosen meant to be well read, for it was a tradition that turned all its reading into writing—and without "let or hinderance." Hence, while della Casa's writing about sodomy may suggest a sterile sexuality, to be equated with his tartuffery as presented in volume V, an ambiguity persistently interweaves della Casa's demons with the fecund ones of Rabelais, and hence tends to celebrate the inclusion of any subject as within the realm of authorial freedom. Once again, the *"extreams* of DELICACY, and the *beginnings* of CONCUPISCENCE" are united.

It is amply obvious that Sterne was never interested in straight-line narrative; indeed, it is perhaps what he most feared, the drying up of the satiric or anatomical vein that enabled him to enrich his pages with endless digressiveness and exuberance, to be the legitimate heir of Petronius, Rabelais, and Swift. The threat of the Warburtonian censor was a trial, to be sure; it paled, however, before the danger to his book that, as a reader, Sterne would find himself lacking. In d'Estella and della Casa, he locates this dilemma, lodging within their questionable presence all his fears that the "discipline, compactness, simplicity, [and] restraint" that "all artists demand of themselves" would destroy the "squirrel soul" that kept him, as a reader and writer, committed to exploration rather than certainty. At the same time, however, they also suggest, in their tenuous existence as learned citations, Sterne's fear that his "squirrel soul" and "baroque depraved imagination" would never match the "discipline" of the satiric voices he emulated, most particularly, their unswerving capacity to measure and judge the follies before them by means of a seemingly inexhaustible and encyclopedic fund of wit and wisdom. Tartuffery, then, is really a twofold enemy for Sterne. On the one hand, we have its common manifestation as the political or social censorship of so-called offensive ideas or values; sexual wit, especially from a cleric, was deemed particularly offensive, but one suspects Warburton was just as offended, for example, by Sterne's attack on polemic divinity, a mode of theological debate with which he strongly identified. That Warburton's motives are ambiguous is precisely the point: any society, at any time and in any place, can exercise tartuffery by finding offensive the word "*whiskers.*" Every word, says Nietzsche, "is a prejudice" (*Human*, 323). Every word is also an imposition of power, an attempt to control or persuade or enforce—although sometimes under the gentler rubrics of "delicacy," "manners," "decorum," and similar words that urge adaptation to "normative" or "correct" social values. There is a sexual prudery that we all know about, but there is an equally dangerous prudery about ideas in general that we often ignore; if the first corrupts our lives through the hypocrisies and deviations of repression, the other corrupts our minds by preventing that "free, fearless hovering over men, customs, laws and the traditional evaluations of things" (*Human*, 30), which Nietzsche identifies with truth-seeking and the "art of reading well."

On the other hand, every individual reading is also an exercise of censorship, every reader (and the author as reader) is a Tartuffe, in so far as reading absorbs the unique text within our own personal system of comprehension. We may resist certain decorums of society, but only because we create a text compatible with other decorums. It is difficult to choose the more narrow reader: the person who follows all the promptings of society ("mystic community"), or the person who pays heed only to the voice of the self ("windy individualism"). Every reading, in short, entails great cost, the sacrifice of other readings to the one at hand; it is not possible, either as writer or reader, to "speak without prejudice." The romantic dream of inclusivity, the skeptical paradise of free and fearless hovering, the soaring above "discipline, compactness, simplicity, restraint in motion and deportment" are all evasions of the demands of the self for certainty and security in confrontation with the otherness of the world.

As much as he seems to have scorned Warburton's attempts to censor *Tristram Shandy*, Sterne knew that the real threat and challenge to his work was his own weakness: the growing exhaustion and enervation that returns the hovering body to certainties and saps one's capacity to "read, read, read, read" (III.36.226/268) all that has to be read. Warburton, ironically enough, was one of the great polymaths of the age, whose attempt to censor Sterne was contradicted by his own energetic resistance to any selectiveness in his own learning and writing. Sterne's great confrontation in writing *Tristram Shandy* was with the simple human desire to rest with what one thinks one knows or understands or has mastered, to adapt to the decorums and values of one's own time and place. Paradoxically, to overcome these natural and compelling tendencies to adapt and to rest requires the greatest "restraint in motion and deportment," as Nietzsche always recognized. The writer of a treatise for "free spirits" was known to labor meticulously over the nuances of each sentence, each word; as a stylist, discipline and compactness are his most distinguishing characteristics. Like Sterne, Nietzsche remained a classicist, trained in the notion that the initial effort is never as good as the second. This distrust of initial impulses suggests to them both that the most difficult human struggle is not to find the meaning of things, but to withhold meaning. The indeterminateness of language, of life itself, is never a sufficient bar to the human need to interpret, to fix and solidify, to make certain. Critical "undecisiveness," the characteristic of the good reader according to Nietzsche, is what corrects that first impulse and is the crown and glory of our moral, aesthetic, and intellectual life. *The disciplined thinker is not the one who controls the flow and reception of diverse and disparate ideas, but the one who does not.*

Let us contemplate the one page of *Tristram Shandy* that might seem free from the two modes of censorship I discuss, the blank page in volume VI. Tristram praises the page with a significant eye toward tartuffian critics: "Thrice happy book! thou wilt have one page, at least, within thy covers, which MALICE will not blacken, and which IGNORANCE cannot misrepresent" (VI.38. 472/568). Recent readers have joined in this praise of blankness, finding in the page an invitation for readers to participate in the writing of *Tristram Shandy*, an invitation that seems to suggest Sterne's postmodernism. Perhaps the blank page is really a mirror: surely it reflects with absolute clarity the fondest dream of the modern theorist, an author who does not merely tolerate, but welcomes the invasive activities of the commentator. Here is censorship at the very edge of absolute power: we can make even a blank page speak our own favorite prejudice!

The blank page is not as empty as it appears, however. It does not occur at a point in the book, say, between chapters 21 and 22 of Volume III, where it might seem totally detached from context; nor does Sterne, with every copy of the work, provide a loose blank sheet for us to insert where we would. Like the words "nose" and "whiskers," the blank page occurs in a context; it is introduced by text preceding it and is commented on afterward. The printer must place it in chapter 38 of volume VI, the reader must find it at that sequential point; the limits on readerly participation seem very persuasive. Moreover, we are specifically instructed as to its intended contents: "call for pen and ink—here's paper ready to your hand.——Sit down, Sir, paint her [the widow Wadman] to your own mind——as like to your mistress as you can——as unlike your wife as your conscience will let you—'tis all one to me——please but your own fancy in it" (VI.38.470/566). Not only is the blank page given a fixed position, but we are instructed in the course of completing the page to chose between desire and conscience, a fundamental Christian *division* out of which—in this reading, at any rate—much of *Tristram Shandy* emerges. Yet, despite Sterne's encouragement of readerly fecundity, I have never come across a copy of the work in which someone has written or even sketched on the blank page.

One reason for this creative failure is simply that the blank page is so highly determined, so incapable of significant division. The only person who might possibly respond precisely as Tristram asks is the male adulterer who is either indifferent to or protected from discovery. The female adulterer is not invited to compare her lover to her husband, although the joke might legitimately have taken that direction—nor is it addressed to the third party in the implied triangle. Tristram's earlier convening of the "*extreams* of DELICACY, and the *beginnings* of CONCUPISCENCE" to sit in judgment on the "whiskers" episode, is here reconvened to measure the married man's response to the work's object of desire: "For never did thy eyes behold, or thy concupiscence covet any thing in this world, more concupiscible than widow *Wadman*" (VI.37.469/565). That we cannot respond, cannot read even a blank page without the falsifications of tartuffery (that is, of interpretation), cannot inscribe it without pangs of conscience, or refuse to inscribe it without anthems of moral rectitude, might be one of Sterne's purposes in providing the opportunity; not only is every word a prejudice, but many blank spaces as well.

The blank page differs little from pages with print, not because words are meaningless or inadequate or indeterminate, but because the urge to define and explain and interpret is indeed "human, all too human." My own analysis is a demonstration of this overwhelming tartuffery. Despite some intellectual commitment to the notion that we must remain forever suspended above (or below) interpretation, that we can no more fix words and meanings into stable relationships than we can fix or make permanent our bodily existence, the urge to "fill in the blank" is not merely overwhelming, but inescapable. I cannot confront the blank page without "reading" it, without reducing its "otherness" to something I can comprehend and incorporate within my own horizon. I recognize—as it seems other readers also have recognized—that I cannot "read" the page by writing into Sterne's work, either by drawing the widow Wadman or describing her. I must write my own work, as Sterne has clearly written his.

Sterne's final use of the word *tartuffery* appears in a letter he wrote to an American correspondent, Dr. John Eustace, a month before his death: the subject is *Tristram Shandy* and a two-handled walking stick that Eustace had sent to Sterne as a token of appreciation: "Your walking stick is in no sense more *shandaic* than in that of its having *more handles than one*—The parallel breaks only in this, that in using the stick, every one will take the handle which suits his convenience. In *Tristram Shandy*, the handle is taken which suits their passions, their ignorance or sensibility." What is often ignored by postmodernists citing this passage is Sterne's lack of sympathy with this notion of multiple handles to his work: "There is so little true feeling," he continues, "in the *herd* of the *world*, that I wish I could have got an act of parliament, when the books first appear'd, 'that none but wise men should look into them.' It is too much to write books and find heads to understand them. The world, however, seems to come into a better temper about them, the people of genius here being, to a man, on its side. . . . A few Hypocrites and Tartufe's, whose approbation could do it nothing but dishonor, remain unconverted" (*Letters*, 411). Wolfgang Iser begins the epilogue to his study of *Tristram Shandy* with portions of this letter, and then attempts a paraphrase: "Evidently his work offers different handles, and one ought to try to grasp them all, not just those which suit one's own disposition. Grasping several handles at once would entail not imposing one's own projections on to the work, but instead allowing the work to correct one's projections. Understanding would then mean absorbing something into oneself that had hitherto not been in the orbit of the reader."[9]

Iser moves on to condemn readers such as Samuel Richardson for failing to heed these precepts and to praise Jean Paul (and Coleridge), "who set Sterne's humour in a new perspective, releasing it from the satirical and ironic constraints which such well-wishers as Burke had imposed on it" (Iser, 123). The other critic who is praised is Nietzsche, who found in *Tristram*'s "fractured form," according to Iser, "the double meaning, the thwarting of expectations [which] turns the reader against his own preconceptions . . . and the pronounced artificiality of representation [which] makes appearance into an ultimate reality. In Sterne, Nietzsche finds his most cherished intentions fulfilled—here is reflected the reverse side of what is. Something must always be questioned if not completely decomposed in order to give expression to what exceeds verbalisation" (Iser, 127). In brief, Iser believes that Nietzsche found in *Tristram Shandy* exactly the same book he finds and has just described to us in the first 120 pages of *his Tristram Shandy*. If Sterne's work has *many* handles, there is no question in Iser's mind about which is the "right" one.

And yet, much if not everything in this study is written in direct disagreement with Iser's reading, beginning, obviously, with his curt dismissal of Edmund Burke's recognition of Sterne's satiric roots. Note carefully in his praise of Jean Paul the rhetorical ploys by which questions about genre and alternative readings become certainties: "releasing" and "constraints," for example, take for granted that a satiric reading is more limited, less valid, than a romantic one, which is, of course, what needs to be demonstrated; while "imposed on it" (Burke's reading) implies a false interpretation, as opposed to Jean Paul's and Iser's readings, which are presumably "found" *in* the text— that is, are really coincident with the text, and hence need not be "imposed." Iser is, in rhetorical terms, begging the question.

It is not surprising to find a book of critical interpretation using these rhetorical modes of persuasion; this study also uses them, although, I hope, with a bit more subtlety. We are, in fact, unable to "read" the world without adopting just such persuasive rhetorics. What is disturbing is Iser's blindness to the one-sidedness (hobby-horsicality) of his own discourse, his inability to see his own implication in his reading of the "many handles" passage. Anyone who has read Iser's previous scholarship on "reader-response" theory will immediately recognize that he has quite literally read *Tristram* as a book written to support that theory. Far from correcting Iser's ideas, Sterne is imagined to be the archetypal reader-response critic (Iser's "school" or "system" of critical theory), and nothing in Iser's reading suggests even a minute widening of his previous orbit. Indeed, even his reading of Sterne's letter suggests the problem; although Iser grabs hold of the meaning he is fondest of, namely, that a text has multiple meanings dependent on the reader, he fails to hear Sterne's powerful condemnation of those who have *not* read *Tristram* "correctly." Iser gives great lip service to multiple readings, but his own criticism is monolithic and decisive.

Tristram Shandy, I suggest, is about the contradiction Iser does not recognize, even—or especially—in his own work. Sterne's letter might easily suggest to another reader quite the opposite of multiple readings because, on one side, is the *herd*, whose "passions," and "ignorance," the result of hypocrisy and tartuffery, induce a misreading of the book, while, on the other, is a reader with a head to "understand" it, a person of genius, to be sure. The word *herd* has uncanny echoes in Nietzsche's work, but even without them one senses that when Sterne read his own book he found in it (or "imposed" on it) some meaning. Like Nietzsche (and Iser, for that matter), Sterne recognized, in his skeptical mode, that the art of reading well was to suspend interpretation, to exercise "caution, patience, subtlety," and to eschew decisiveness in favor of hovering among alternatives. But also like Nietzsche (and unlike Iser), Sterne had no delusions about the strength of the reader's need to falsify the "facts" in order to establish meaning, the reader's (inevitable) tendency to lose patience and subtlety in the drive to "force every event in nature into an hypothesis" (IX.32.644/804). Sterne's satire, like Nietzsche's philosophy, is directed against the hypocrisy (gravity) and tartuffery by which we hide this need and its results from ourselves and from others: as readers of books and people and the world, we are *all* and *always* mounted and galloping. The emphasis of Sterne's letter is not on a toleration of multiple readings, as Iser believes, but on the *misreadings* of those—all of us—who allow the hobby-horse to dominate; it is, in short, Sterne's "human, all too human," response to his belief that he had been misunderstood.

I do agree with Iser that Nietzsche "finds his most cherished intentions fulfilled" in Sterne, but would immediately complicate that statement—as I have suggested in this chapter—by suggesting that it is Iser's reading of Nietzsche's intentions that is "imposed" on Sterne's text, that not only is Iser's Sterne not my Sterne, but his Nietzsche is not my Nietzsche. Iser's last sentence quoted above offers a good illustration: "Something must always be questioned if not completely decomposed in order to give expression to what exceeds verbalisation." I find this a rather romantic *misreading* of Nietzsche, positing as it does a teleological resting point, a "truth" that will emerge beyond "verbalisation"; the sentence also contains an unexamined "moral imperative" in the word *must*. The blank page of *Tristram Shandy* seems to me a useful comment on the "dream of order" behind Iser's sentence, a dream both Sterne and Nietzsche reject—although with an irony that feeds Iser's misreading. I might suggest that Iser's sentence would be more compatible with Sterne and Nietzsche were it rewritten: "Some things ought never be questioned, never completely decomposed, if we ever hope to give presence [a much more useful word than *expression* in this context] to what exceeds human language." For Sterne, those "things" constitute his Christian core of belief, under multiple questioning, multiple threat of "decomposition" in mid-eighteenth-century Europe; *Tristram Shandy*, as a satire, alerts us to the danger of losing that core. One hundred years later, Nietzsche found the tartuffian moral world that Sterne had predicted would be the outcome of that loss. His response is not, as Iser assumes, a celebration of the freedoms thus gained, but a lament over the hypocrisy and tartuffery that creates "dreams of freedom" on the ruins of Christianity, dreams Nietzsche found as falsifying as any of the "dreams of order" they replaced.

Is my reading correct—or Iser's? Mine, naturally enough. It would be ridiculous to suggest otherwise, and my reading of Sterne and Nietzsche has taught me that two particular modern pieties—that both readings are equally correct, or that the reading is correct for me, but not for Iser or any other reader—are "errant bits of tartuffery," believed by no one. Our interpretations are our lives, and we invest enormous stakes of psychic pleasure and security in their well-being. We can hardly speak five words on any given subject before we begin to exercise persuasiveness, and the health of our ideas seems always to depend on the agreement of others. If we are fortunate, our differences will not lead to war and bloodshed—no differences of opinion about *Tristram Shandy* have ever done so. But the drive to find meaning even in the blank page is the same instinct that does send countries to war, and our understanding of this drive has become the most urgent necessity for a century dominated by demagoguery.

To remain undecisive in our interpretations is the most difficult goal we can set for ourselves, one that we violate with almost every word we speak, just as Christians of past centuries violated their moral codes with almost every motion of their bodies. Virtue and undecisiveness are defined by the human inadequacy in achieving either, and to elide that difficulty by suggesting an idealistic embrace of academic impartiality or universal tolerance is simply the opening gambit of an often successful rhetorical strategy in defense of conviction. Nietzsche speaks to the point with his usual aphoristic brilliance in *Human, All Too Human*: "It is not conflict of opinions that has made history so violent but conflict of belief in opinions, that is to say conflict of convictions" (*Human*, 199–200). Readers of *Tristram Shandy* will immediately recognize the sentiment as an offspring of Sterne's motto to volumes I and II of *Tristram Shandy*: "Men are tormented with the Opinions they have of Things, and not by the Things themselves." But even that neat concurrence of views, coming on the last leaf of this reading, should not deceive us into a belief that we have arrived, finally, at a valid understanding of the Nietzschean Sterne. The straight line of conviction is always the danger we must most fear, even when—especially when—we are on the verge of embracing, wholeheartedly, the notion that convictions "are more dangerous enemies of truth than lies" (*Human*, 179). It is far better, but also far more difficult, not to be convinced by that argument either. Perhaps another Nietzschean aphorism, from the voice of Zarathustra, speaks better to what *Tristram Shandy* might mean:

> "That I have to be struggle and becoming and goal and conflict of goals; ah, he who divines my will surely divines, too, along what *crooked* paths it has to go!" (*Zarathustra*, 138).

Notes and References

1. The Milieu of *Tristram Shandy*

1. L. P. Curtis, *The Politicks of Laurence Sterne* (Oxford: Oxford University Press, 1929); and Kenneth Monkman, "More of Sterne's Politicks, 1741–42," *The Shandean* 1 (1989):53–108; "Sterne and the '45 (1743–48)," *The Shandean* 2 (1990):45–136; and "Sterne's Farewell to Politics," *The Shandean* 3 (1991):98–125.

2. The best study of eighteenth-century sentimentalism is that by John Mullan in *Sentiment and Sociability: The Language of Feeling in the Eighteenth Century* (Oxford: Clarendon Press, 1988).

2. The Importance of *Tristram Shandy*

1. Herbert Read was perhaps the first to connect Sterne and Keats: "We know that Keats was familiar with *Tristram Shandy*, and it may be that his notion of *Negative Capability* . . . owes something to Sterne's character of Yorick—in any case, Sterne was certainly also 'a man . . . capable of being in uncertainties, Mysteries, doubts'" (*The Contrary Experience* [London: Faber & Faber, 1963], 330). Keats outlined his idea in a letter to his brothers dated 21 December 1817; I have normalized the text.

3. *Tristram Shandy* among the Critics

1. Alan B. Howes, ed. *Sterne: The Critical Heritage* (London: Routledge & Kegan Paul, 1974), 147; hereafter cited in text. Howes gathers many of these early responses and I have relied heavily upon him in this chapter.

2. Heinrich Heine, "The Romantic School," in *The Prose Writings*, trans. S. L. Fleishman (London: W. Scott, 1887), 130–31.

3. Quoted in Peter Rudy, "Lev Tolstoj's Apprenticeship to Laurence Sterne," *Slavic and East European Journal* 15 (1971):11.

4. Friedrich Nietzsche, *Human, All Too Human: A Book for Free Spirits*, trans. R. J. Hollingdale (Cambridge: Cambridge University Press, 1986), 238–39; hereafter cited in text as *Human*.

5. *The Great Tradition* (London: Chatto & Windus, 1948), 2, n. 2.

6. Wilbur L. Cross, *The Life and Times of Laurence Sterne* 3d ed. (New Haven, Conn.: Yale University Press, 1929); Lewis Perry Curtis, ed. *Letters of Laurence Sterne* (Oxford: Clarendon Press, 1935); hereafter cited in text as *Letters*. Cross's work has been superseded by a biography in two volumes by Arthur H. Cash, *Laurence Sterne: The Early and Middle Years* and *The Later Years* (London: Methuen, 1975, 1986).

7. John Traugott, *Tristram Shandy's World: Sterne's Philosophical Rhetoric* (Berkeley: University of California Press, 1954).

8. James E. Swearingen, *Reflexivity in "Tristram Shandy": An Essay in Phenomenological Criticism* (New Haven, Conn.: Yale University Press, 1977); Wolfgang Iser, *Tristram Shandy* (Cambridge: Cambridge University Press, 1988).

9. D. W. Jefferson, "*Tristram Shandy* and the Tradition of Learned Wit," *Essays in Criticism* 1 (1951):225–48; Wayne C. Booth, "The Self-Conscious Narrator in Comic Fiction before *Tristram Shandy*," *PMLA* 67 (1952):163–85.

10. John M. Stedmond, *The Comic Art of Laurence Sterne: Convention and Innovation in "Tristram Shandy" and "A Sentimental Journey"* (Toronto: University of Toronto Press, 1967); Melvyn New, *Laurence Sterne as Satirist: A Reading of "Tristram Shandy"* (Gainesville: University of Florida Press, 1969). Both studies found their impetus for a reconsideration of the genre question in Northrop Frye, *Anatomy of Criticism: Four Essays* (Princeton, N.J.: Princeton University Press, 1957).

11. The feminist debate opened with a fine essay by Leigh A. Ehlers, "Mrs. Shandy's 'Lint and Basilicon': The Importance of Women in *Tristram Shandy*," *South Atlantic Review* 46 (1981):61–75. See also, Helen Ostovich, "Reader as Hobby-Horse in *Tristram Shandy*," *Philological Quarterly* 68 (1989):325–42; H. W. Matalene, "Sexual Scripting in Montaigne and Sterne," *Comparative Literature* 41 (1989):360–77; Melvyn New, "Job's Wife and Sterne's Other Women," in *Out of Bounds: Male Writers and Engender(ed) Criticism*, ed. E. Langland and L. Claridge (Amherst: University of Massachusetts Press, 1990), 55–74; Calvin Thomas, "*Tristram Shandy's* Consent to Incompleteness: Discourse, Disavowal, Disruption," *Literature and Psychology* 36 (1990):44–62; and Paula Loscocco, "'Can't Live Without 'Em': Walter Shandy and the Woman Within," *Eighteenth Century: Theory and Interpretation* 32 (1991):166–79. For a totally unsympathetic reading of Sterne see Ruth Perry, "Words for Sex: The Verbal-Sexual Continuum in *Tristram Shandy*," *Studies in the Novel* 20 (1988):27–42; for a healthy correc-

Notes and References

tive to that essay's ill will, see Juliet McMaster, "Walter Shandy, Sterne, and Gender: A Feminist Foray," *English Studies in Canada* 15 (1989):441–58.

12. Jonathan Lamb, *Sterne's Fiction and the Double Principle* (Cambridge: Cambridge University Press, 1989).

13. Seon Givens, ed., *James Joyce: Two Decades of Criticism* (New York: Vanguard Press, 1948), 11–12.

14. "The Theme of the Joseph Novels" in *Thomas Mann's Addresses: Delivered at the Library of Congress, 1942–1949* (Washington, D.C.: Library of Congress, 1963), 12–13.

4. Introduction

1. Stuart Gilbert, *James Joyce's Ulysses: A Study*, 2d ed. (New York: Vintage Books, 1952).

2. *Twilight of the Idols*, trans. R. J. Hollingdale (Harmondsworth: Penguin, 1968), 44; hereafter cited in text.

5. Satire

1. Friedrich Nietzsche, *Thus Spoke Zarathustra*, trans. R. J. Hollingdale (Harmondsworth: Penguin, 1961), 212; hereafter cited in text as *Zarathustra*.

2. See Melvyn New, "Sterne's Rabelaisian Fragment: A Text from the Holograph Manuscript," *PMLA* 87 (1972):1083–92.

3. Shakespeare, *Hamlet*, V.l.184–85.

4. *Sermons of the Late Reverend Laurence Sterne* (London, 1769) VI:166–68; hereafter cited in text as *Sermons*.

5. See "Verses on the Death of Dr Swift, D.S.P.D.," 11. 315–16: "His vein, ironically grave, / Exposed the fool, and lashed the knave" (*The Complete Poems*, ed. Pat Rogers [London: Penguin, 1983]), 493.

6. "Epistle to Arbuthnot," 11. 75–80, in *The Poems of Alexander Pope*, ed. John Butt (New Haven, Conn.: Yale University Press, 1963), 600.

7. Horace, *Satire I.10*.

8. Smith Palmer Bovie, trans. *Satires and Epistles of Horace* (Chicago: University of Chicago Press, 1959), 122.

9. There is, of course, satire that is anti-institutional, although still judgmental and discriminatory; one almost always discovers, however, that such satire pits one institution against another, or an ideal institution against its perceived corruption. The ideal of individual judgment or revolutionary change as the final arbiter seems inimical to satire, because the inadequacy of individual reason is always one of satire's most obvious targets.

10. "On the Testimony of Conscience," *Sermons*, in *Prose Works*, ed. Louis Landa (Oxford: Basil Blackwell, 1963), IX:150; hereafter cited in text.

11. See, for example, the theory of vapors in section IX of *Tale of a Tub*, eds. Angus Ross and David Woolley (Oxford: Oxford University Press, 1986), 77–79; hereafter cited in text.

12. The best introduction to the ideas glanced at in this paragraph is Richard H. Popkin, *The History of Scepticism from Erasmus to Spinoza* (Berkeley: University of California Press, 1979). The best application of these ideas to Sterne is by Donald R. Wehrs, "Sterne, Cervantes, Montaigne: Fideistic Skepticism and the Rhetoric of Desire," *Comparative Literature Studies* 25 (1988):127–51.

13. Adam Smith, *The Theory of Moral Sentiments*, eds. D. D. Raphael and A. L. Macfie (Oxford: Clarendon Press, 1976), 9.

6. Heads

1. James A. Work shaped a generation's attitude toward Mrs. Shandy with these comments: "My mother indeed, though she appears rarely, says little, and has 'no character at all,' is one of the most delightful of Sterne's creations. . . . [S]he is chiefly notable for her inability—or lack of desire—to say anything for herself" ("Introduction" to *Tristram Shandy* [New York: Odyssey Press, 1940], lvi–lvii).

2. See *Notes*, 51–52, n. to 8.1–3. My own favorite hint, in the bed of justice (VI.18), is discussed in chapter 8.

3. See *Notes*, 44, n. to 2.19ff.

4. The primary studies of this aspect of Sterne are Peter Conrad, *Shandyism: The Character of Romantic Irony* (New York: Barnes and Noble, 1978); and Marshall Brown, "Sterne's Stories," in *Preromanticism* (Stanford, Calif.: Stanford University Press, 1991), 261–300.

5. See the fine essay by Arthur H. Cash, "The Birth of Tristram Shandy: Sterne and Dr. Burton," in *Studies in the Eighteenth Century*, ed. R. F. Brissenden (Canberra: Australian National University Press, 1968), 233–54.

6. John Dryden, "MacFlecknoe," l. 6.

7. Donald Greene, "Pragmatism versus Dogmatism: The Ideology of *Tristram Shandy*," in *Approaches to Teaching Sterne's "Tristram Shandy*," ed. Melvyn New (New York: Modern Language Association of America, 1989), 106; 110, n. 1.

8. D. W. Jefferson, "*Tristram Shandy* and the Tradition of Learned Wit," in *Essays in Criticism* 1 (1951):225–48.

9. Jonathan Lamb, *Sterne's Fiction and the Double Principle* (Cambridge: Cambridge University Press, 1989), deals extensively with subjects raised by Nietzsche's mode of thinking, but we have quite different read-

ings of *Tristram*, beginning with a difference of opinion as to whether the "tremendous error" of human language is a cause for celebration or repair.

7. Hearts

1. Friedrich Nietzsche, *On the Genealogy of Morals*, trans. Walter Kaufmann (New York: Vintage Books, 1969), 19.

2. John Traugott, *Tristram Shandy's World: Sterne's Philosophical Rhetoric* (Berkeley: University of California Press, 1954).

3. John Traugott, ed., *Laurence Sterne: A Collection of Critical Essays* (Englewood Cliffs, N.J.: Prentice-Hall, 1968), 4.

4. Friedrich Nietzsche, *Untimely Meditations*, trans. R. J. Hollingdale (Cambridge: Cambridge University Press, 1983), 27–36 and passim.

5. See John Mullan, *Sentiment and Sociability: The Language of Feeling in the Eighteenth Century* (Oxford: Clarendon Press, 1988).

6. Nineteenth-century editors often altered the spelling to *Le Fevre* to reduce the sting of Sterne's original spelling; to be sure, two occurrences in the first edition of volume IX also use that spelling.

7. See *Notes*, 39–40, n. to 1.1ff.

8. Pierre Charron, *Of Wisdome*, trans. Samson Lennard (1612), 83, 85 (bk. 1, chap. 22).

9. They point out (*Notes*, 550–51, n. to 806.15–16) that no similar passage occurs in Charron, although Plato is an obvious choice; Diogenes seems more problematic, but they find one of his recorded observations apropos. "Being asked what was the right time to marry, Diogenes replied, 'For a young man not yet: for an old man never at all.'"

10. It has been noted that the wavy line looks like eighteenth-century representations of spermatozoa under the microscope.

11. Sterne, *A Sentimental Journey*, ed. Gardner D. Stout (Berkeley: University of California Press, 1967), 153; hereafter cited in text as *Journey*.

12. The best discussion of sexual punning in *Tristram* is perhaps that by Frank Brady, "*Tristram Shandy*: Sexuality, Morality, and Sensibility," *Eighteenth-Century Studies* 4 (1970):41–56. See also my short essay "'At the backside of the door of purgatory': A Note on Annotating *Tristram Shandy*," in *Laurence Sterne: Riddles and Mysteries*, ed. Valerie G. Myer (London and New York: Vision and Barnes and Noble, 1984), 15–23.

13. Miguel de Cervantes, *Don Quixote*, trans. Peter Motteux, rev. John Ozell (New York: Random House, 1950), 324–26 (I.IV.10); the current discussion is based on materials in *Notes*, 431–34.

14. Robert Burton, *The Anatomy of Melancholy*, ed. Floyd Dell and Paul Jordan-Smith (New York: Tudor Publishing Company, 1941), 45–50.

8. Joy

1. Friedrich Nietzsche, *Beyond Good and Evil*, trans. Marianne Cowan (Chicago: Henry Regnery, 1955), 86.

2. *South Atlantic Review* 46 (1981):61–75. A shorter version of the essay appears in *Approaches to Teaching Sterne's "Tristram Shandy,"* 118–22. In the same volume, see also Elizabeth W. Harries, "The Sorrows and Confessions of a Cross-Eyed 'Female-Reader' of Sterne," 111–17.

3. *Philological Quarterly* 68 (1989):325–42.

4. For students interested in these questions, see other readings listed above, n. 11 to chap. 3.

5. Ruth Perry, "Words for Sex: The Verbal-Sexual Continuum in *Tristram Shandy,*" *Studies in the Novel* 20 (1988):27–42.

6. I oversimplify important issues here, not least the classical notion of suspension, the belief that "something" can be known, but the refusal to accept any particular "something" as knowable.

7. My tendency to see *self* and *other* in terms of male and female follows Sterne's lead; the emphasis on procreation in *Tristram* creates definite boundaries. In *A Sentimental Journey*, these boundaries tend to fade, and in "Job's Wife and Sterne's Other Women" (in *Out of Bounds: Male Writers and Engender(ed) Criticism*, ed. E. Langland and L. Claridge [Amherst: University of Massachusetts Press, 1990], 55–74), I suggest the possibility of genderless union.

8. Charles Kerby-Miller, ed. *Memoirs of Martinus Scriblerus* (New Haven, Conn.: Yale University Press, 1950), chap. 5.

9. J. Paul Hunter, "Clocks, Calendars, and Names: The Troubles of Tristram and the Aesthetics of Uncertainty," in *Rhetorics of Order/Ordering Rhetorics in English Neoclassical Literature*, eds. J. Douglas Canfield and J. Paul Hunter (Newark: Delaware University Press, 1989), 173–98.

10. See Arthur H. Cash, *Laurence Sterne: The Early and Middle Years* (London: Methuen, 1975), 243–61, for a full discussion of Sterne's career as a "commissary" (that is, judge) in the spiritual courts of the Anglican Church.

11. See *Letters*, 74 (to Robert Dodsley, 23 May 1759): "The Plan . . . is a most extensive one,—taking in, not only, the Weak part of the Sciences, in wch the true point of Ridicule lies—but every Thing else, which I find Laugh-at-able in my way."

12. *Zarathustra*, 68. Nietzsche continues: "And when I beheld my devil, I found him serious, thorough, profound, solemn: it was the Spirit of Gravity—through him all things are ruined. One does not kill by anger but by laughter. Come, let us kill the Spirit of Gravity!"

Notes and References

9. Tartuffery

1. See, especially, *The Will to Power*, trans. Walter Kaufmann and R. J. Hollingdale (New York: Vintage, 1968), sections 98–101.

2. *MLN* 103 (1988):1053.

3. *The Will to Power*, 174 (section 315). The other citations from this work are on pages 173, 229, 17, and 114, respectively; from *Beyond Good and Evil*, pages 5, 28, and 184.

4. Melvyn New, "Sterne, Warburton, and the Burden of Exuberant Wit," *Eighteenth-Century Studies* 15 (1982):245–74.

5. Typically enough, Sterne parodies the advice by having Trim describe Tristram's accident with the window sash, "so that priests and virgins might have listened to it" (V.20.379/453); it is this sort of private reference that seems to have fueled Warburton's animosity.

6. These translations are taken from *Notes*, 337.

7. *Notes*, 343, n. to 414.13–14. The passage is from *Contempt of the World and the Vanities Thereof*, trans. George Cotton (3d ed. [1622], 439).

8. See New, "Sterne, Warburton," 265 and n. 49.

9. Wolfgang Iser, *Tristram Shandy* (Cambridge: Cambridge University Press, 1988), 121; hereafter cited in text.

Selected Bibliography

Primary Sources

Editions of *Tristram Shandy*

Work, James A., ed. New York: Odyssey-Macmillan, 1940.

Watt, Ian, ed. Boston: Houghton, Mifflin, 1965.

Petrie, Graham, ed. Baltimore: Penguin, 1967.

Florida Edition of the Works of Laurence Sterne, The. Vols. I and II, *The Text of Tristram Shandy.* Eds. Melvyn New and Joan New. Vol. III. *The Notes to Tristram Shandy.* Eds. Melvyn New, with Richard A. Davies and W. G. Day. Gainesville: University Press of Florida, 1978, 1984.

Anderson, Howard, ed. New York: Norton, 1980.

Ross, Ian Campbell, ed. Oxford: Oxford University Press, 1983.

Other Sterne Works

A Political Romance. Facsimile rpt. Menston, UK: Scolar, 1971.

Curtis, Lewis Perry, ed. *Letters of Laurence Sterne.* Oxford: Clarendon, 1935.

Cross, Wilbur L., ed. *Works.* 12 vols. New York: Taylor, 1904.

Jack, Ian, ed., *A Sentimental Journey,* with *A Political Romance* and "Journal to Eliza." London: Oxford University Press, 1968.

New, Melvyn, ed. "Sterne's Rabelaisian Fragment: A Text from the Holograph Manuscript." *PMLA* 87 (1972):1083–92.

Stout, Jr., Gardner D., ed. *A Sentimental Journey through France and Italy.* Berkeley: University of California Press, 1967.

Works. 7 vols. Oxford and Boston: Blackwell and Houghton, 1926–27.

Secondary Sources

Books and Parts of Books

Brown, Marshall. "Sterne's Stories," 261–300. In *Preromanticism*. Stanford, Calif.: Stanford University Press, 1991. If one can accept the notion that romanticism is a rejection of rationalism, much of Brown's argument that Sterne is preromantic follows; it is, however, a premise of some dubiety.

Byrd, Max. *Tristram Shandy*. London: George Allen & Unwin, 1985. A work designed primarily for students; it moves through *Tristram* volume by volume and contains a discussion of recent criticism. Because Byrd and I agree only about half the time, his study may be a useful counterbalance to mine.

Cash, Arthur H. *Laurence Sterne: The Early and Middle Years*. London: Methuen, 1975.

———. *Laurence Sterne: The Later Years*. London: Methuen, 1986. The two-volume standard and definitive biography of Sterne.

——— and John M. Stedmond, eds. *The Winged Skull: Papers from the Laurence Sterne Bicentenary Conference*. Kent State, Ohio: Kent State University Press, 1971. Eighteen essays and other useful material. Worth singling out are Kenneth Monkman on "Sterne, Hamlet, and Yorick" and R. F. Brissenden's reconsideration of Wayne Booth's "Did Sterne Complete *Tristram Shandy?*"

Erickson, Robert A. "*Tristram Shandy* and the Womb of Speculation," 193–248. In *Mother Midnight: Birth, Sex, and Fate in Eighteenth-Century Fiction*. New York: AMS Press, 1986. Erickson weaves an imaginative web from Sterne's interest in procreation, midwifery, writing, and death, arguing that *Tristram Shandy* is a self-examination into origins and identity.

Holtz, William V. *Image and Immortality: A Study of "Tristram Shandy."* Providence, R.I.: Brown University Press, 1970. An interesting discussion of Sterne's relations with Hogarth and Reynolds, and with the tradition of literature as "pictorial" representation.

Lamb, Jonathan. *Sterne's Fiction and the Double Principle*. Cambridge: Cambridge University Press, 1989. Lamb is determined to find *Tristram* an indeterminate text and often ties himself in knots in the effort to mask with involuted prose his reduction of Sterne to a simple "solution." Some parts, however, are worth laboring over.

Lanham, Richard. *"Tristram Shandy": The Games of Pleasure*. Berkeley: University of California Press, 1973. A useful and accessible reading of

Selected Bibliography

Tristram in relation to "game theory," a concept of literature as disinterested play.

Moglen, Helene. *The Philosophical Irony of Laurence Sterne.* Gainesville: University of Florida Press, 1975. An elaboration of Traugott's reading of Tristram as "existential sentimentalism." Locke is the "hero" of a work that uncovers the "nightmare world of alienation and absurdity," a "world without absolutes."

Mullan, John. "Laurence Sterne and the 'Sociality' of the Novel," 147–200. In *Sentiment and Sociability: The Language of Feeling in the Eighteenth Century.* Oxford: Clarendon, 1988. The best study available of a concern vital to *Tristram,* how to understand sentiment and sensibility in the eighteenth century.

Myer, Valerie G., ed. *Laurence Sterne: Riddles and Mysteries.* London and Totowa, N.J.: Vision and Barnes and Noble, 1984. Eleven essays directed primarily toward a student audience. W. G. Day's "Locke May Not Be the Key" is especially useful.

New, Melvyn. *Laurence Sterne as Satirist: A Reading of "Tristram Shandy."* Gainesville: University of Florida Press, 1969. I continue to like my first study of *Tristram,* which suggests that Sterne was quite correct about hobby-horses.

———. "Laurence Sterne," 471–99. In *British Novelists: 1660–1800. Dictionary of Literary Biography,* ed. Martin C. Battestin. Detroit: Gale Research, 1985. Vol. 39, part 2. An introduction to Sterne's life and works.

———, ed. *Approaches to Teaching Sterne's "Tristram Shandy."* New York: The Modern Language Association of America, 1989. Nineteen essays centered on methods of teaching *Tristram* to undergraduates, along with an extensive survey of bibliographical resources and the current state of commentary.

———, ed. *"Tristram Shandy": Contemporary Critical Essays.* "New Casebooks." London and New York: Macmillan and St. Martin's, 1992. Eight essays, a "polemical introduction," and an annotated checklist of further reading.

———. "Swift and Sterne: Two Tales, Several Sermons, and a Relationship Revisited," 164–86. In *Critical Essays on Jonathan Swift,* edited by Frank Palmeri. New York: G. K. Hall, 1993. A discussion of "Slawkenbergius's Tale" against the background of Swift's *Tale of a Tub* and the Anglican faith of Swift and Sterne.

Piper, William Bowman. *Laurence Sterne.* New York: Twayne, 1965. A reading of *Tristram* as a novel, considering the Shandy family as involved in the story of its own survival.

Rothstein, Eric. *"Tristram Shandy,"* 62–108. In *Systems of Order and Inquiry in Later Eighteenth-Century Fiction.* Berkeley: University of California Press, 1975. Rothstein reads *Tristram* as a series of analogies between characters, actions, episodes, relationships, and the like. A fine example of how to read *Tristram* carefully.

Smyth, John Vignaux. "Sterne," 13–98. In *A Question of Eros: Irony in Sterne, Kierkegaard, and Barthes.* Gainesville: University Press of Florida, 1986. A good introduction to the postmodernist reading of Tristram. Smyth is particularly good on the eroticism of the hobby-horse.

Stedmond, John M. *The Comic Art of Laurence Sterne: Convention and Innovation in "Tristram Shandy" and "A Sentimental Journey."* Toronto: University of Toronto Press, 1967. A useful, straightforward account of the issues of genre, style, and satire in the first chapters, followed by a long chapter taking us through *Tristram* volume by volume.

Swearingen, James E. *Reflexivity in "Tristram Shandy": An Essay in Phenomenological Criticism.* New Haven, Conn.: Yale University Press, 1977. The phenomenological approach produces, as it must, a unity in Tristram's mind that explains the entire work.

Traugott, John. *Tristram Shandy's World: Sterne's Philosophical Rhetoric.* Berkeley: University of California Press, 1954. The single work that has most dominated criticism of Tristram over the past four decades. Sterne recognized errors in Locke, most particularly his "despair" over language, and corrected them by showing how feeling can bridge the gap between communications and communicators.

———. *Laurence Sterne: A Collection of Critical Essays.* "Twentieth Century Views." Englewood Cliffs, N.J.: Prentice-Hall, 1968. Reprints several landmarks of Sterne criticism including essays by Benjamin H. Lehman (an early attempt to establish Sterne's philosophical importance) and Viktor Shklovsky, the Russian formalist, who labels *Tristram* the "most typical novel of world literature"—the most misunderstood label in recent criticism of Sterne.

Journal Articles

Booth, Wayne C. "Did Sterne Complete *Tristram Shandy*?" *Modern Philology* 48 (1951):172–83. A well-wrought argument that Sterne knew very early in the book where he was going to end it—that is, with the amours of Uncle Toby, the choicest morsel of the work. Booth posits an author in firm control of his work.

———. "The Self-Conscious Narrator in Comic Fiction before *Tristram Shandy.*" *PMLA* 67 (1952):163–85. Booth links Sterne's narrative voice to earlier narrators in Cervantes, Marivaux, Fielding, and others, all of whom share such devices as address to the audience, digression, and a

Selected Bibliography

sense of writing as performance. Reprinted in New, ed., *Contemporary Critical Essays*.

Brady, Frank. "*Tristram Shandy*: Sexuality, Morality, and Sensibility." *Eighteenth-Century Studies* 4 (1970):41–56. Brady ties together the topics of his title by keeping his ear closely attuned to the sexual innuendoes of Sterne's text, even during its moral and sentimental moments. Reprinted in New, ed., *Contemporary Critical Essays*.

Burckhardt, Sigurd. "*Tristram Shandy*'s Law of Gravity." *ELH* 28 (1961):70–88. A *tour de force* of careful, imaginative attention to the text, with a welcome emphasis on "body" rather than "heart." Burckhardt uses "gravity" as both a physical law and a synonym for seriousness. Reprinted in New, ed., *Contemporary Critical Essays*.

Cash, Arthur H. "The Lockean Psychology of *Tristram Shandy*." *ELH* 22 (1955):125–35. An important corrective arguing the essential difference between modern ideas of "stream of consciousness" and Locke's (Sterne's) concept of the "train of ideas."

Ehlers, Leigh A. "Mrs. Shandy's 'Lint and Basilicon': The Importance of Women in *Tristram Shandy*." *South Atlantic Review* 46 (1981):61–75. Persuasively argues that Elizabeth Shandy is not the negative character of most critical comment but a procreative and restorative force. An innovating scholarly corrective to those who condemn Sterne's attitude toward women.

Harries, Elizabeth W. "Sterne's Novels: Gathering Up the Fragments." *ELH* 49 (1982):35–49. Harries takes a very "modern" theme, the fragmented text, and demonstrates that its scriptural context is as rich, paradoxical, and subtle, as any modern discussion of incompleteness. Reprinted in New, ed., *Contemporary Critical Essays*.

Jefferson, D. W. "*Tristram Shandy* and the Tradition of Learned Wit." *Essays in Criticism* 1 (1951):225–48. Jefferson points the way toward understanding the presence in *Tristram* of a great deal of traditional satire directed against medicine, law, theology, and science—and "unbridled rationalism" in general. Reprinted in New, ed., *Contemporary Critical Essays*.

New, Melvyn. "Sterne, Warburton, and the Burden of Exuberant Wit." *Eighteenth-Century Studies* 15 (1982):245–74. A discussion of Sterne's attempt to imitate the fecundity of wit he associated with Rabelais, Burton, Swift, and the like, and the uses he made of Bishop Warburton's attempts to muzzle that wit in the name of decency.

———. "Sterne and the Narrative of Determinateness." *Eighteenth-Century Fiction* 4 (1992):315–29. An attempt to respond to Jonathan Lamb and others who read *Tristram Shandy* as a postmodernist text that celebrates indeterminacy.

Ostovich, Helen. "Reader as Hobby-horse in *Tristram Shandy.*" *Philological Quarterly* 68 (1989):325–42. A stout defense of Elizabeth Shandy and of woman readers who are able to hold their own against a flawed male perspective. Reprinted in New, ed., *Contemporary Critical Essays.*

Thomas, Calvin. *"Tristram Shandy*'s Consent to Incompleteness: Discourse, Disavowal, Disruption." *Literature and Psychology* 36 (1990):44–62. The psychological ideas of Jacques Lacan are put to good use to analyze the Shandy males.

Wehrs, Donald R. "Sterne, Cervantes, Montaigne: Fideistic Skepticism and the Rhetoric of Desire." *Comparative Literature Studies* 25 (1988):127–51. An important essay that demonstrates how "indeterminacy" in Sterne is tied to classical skepticism—and, through it, to an orthodox Christian acceptance of our indeterminate world. Reprinted in New, ed., *Contemporary Critical Essays.*

Zimmerman, Everett. *"Tristram Shandy* and Narrative Representation." *Eighteenth Century: Theory and Interpretation* 28 (1987):127–47. The influence of secularization on Sterne's sense of language is given concrete reference to concerns of his day: challenges to scriptural authority and increasing demands for historic documentation. Sterne had grave reservations about the loss of faith in the modern world. An important essay. Reprinted in New, ed., *Contemporary Critical Essays.*

Bibliography

Hartley, Lodwick. *Laurence Sterne in the Twentieth Century: An Essay and a Bibliography of Sternean Studies, 1900–1965.* Chapel Hill: University of North Carolina Press, 1966.

———. *Laurence Sterne: An Annotated Bibliography, 1965–1977.* Boston: G. K. Hall, 1978. The standard checklists of criticism; the first collection is more accurate than the second, which was put together in haste and is filled with errors and dubious evaluations.

Howes, Alan B. *Sterne: The Critical Heritage.* London: Routledge, 1974. A useful collection of excerpts of contemporary commentaries on *Tristram* and Sterne's other writings, along with nineteenth-century criticisms from England and Europe.

New, Melvyn. "Surviving the Seventies: Sterne, Collins and Their Recent Critics." *Eighteenth Century: Theory and Interpretation* 25 (1984):3–24. Fills some of the gaps in Hartley's second checklist and extends coverage (not thoroughly, however) through 1980.

(*The Scriblerian*, published semiannually, has included reviews of new books and essays on Sterne since its Spring 1986 issue. *The Shandean: The Annual of the Laurence Sterne Trust* published its first volume in 1989, and will be a mine of biographical and bibliographical information on Sterne in future years.)

Index

149

Index

The Author

Melvyn New, Professor of English at the University of Florida, has been writing on Laurence Sterne for more than 25 years. He is coeditor, with Joan New, of the Florida edition of *Tristram Shandy*, volumes I and II: The Text (1978); and, with Richard A. Davies and W. G. Day, of *Tristram Shandy*, volume III: The Notes (1984). Currently, he is bringing to completion volumes IV and V, an edition of Sterne's sermons. He is the author of *Laurence Sterne as Satirist* (1969) and *Telling New Lies: Essays in Fiction, Past and Present* (1992); and editor of *Approaches to Teaching Sterne's "Tristram Shandy,"* (1989) *"Tristram Shandy": Contemporary Critical Essays* (1992), and *The Complete Novels and Selected Writings of Amy Levy, 1861–1889* (1993). He has published more than 30 essays on Sterne and other eighteenth- and twentieth-century writers in such journals as *PMLA, Philological Quarterly, Modern Fiction Studies, Studies in Bibliography, The Georgia Review, Eighteenth-Century Studies, Eighteenth-Century: Theory and Interpretation, MLN*, and *Eighteenth-Century Fiction*. Professor New also serves as the Sterne-Smollett editor of *The Scriblerian* and the American editor of *The Shandean: The Annual of the Laurence Sterne Trust*. He chaired the Department of English at the University of Florida from 1979 to 1988.